YOUNG PEOPLE'S STORY OF
OUR HERITAGE

YOUNG PEOPLE'S
STORY OF
OUR HERITAGE

THE MODERN WORLD

V. M. HILLYER and E. G. HUEY

New Edition Designed and Revised by Childrens Press, Chicago

Consultants

William T. Nichol, Principal
Charles Gates Dawes Elementary School, Evanston, Illinois

John R. Lee, Professor of Education
Northwestern University, Evanston, Illinois

Meredith Press, New York

Illustrations in the order in which they appear

Library of Congress Catalog Card Number: 66-11331

Copyright © 1966 by Meredith Publishing Company. Originally published under the title of *A Child's History of the World* by V. M. Hillyer. Revised and enlarged Edition, with new material by Edward G. Huey. Copyright, 1924, by The Century Co. Copyright, 1947, by D. Appleton-Century Company, Inc. Copyright, 1951, by Appleton-Century-Crofts, Inc. Copyright, 1952 by Origineale Fletcher. All rights reserved. Printed in the U.S.A. Published simultaneously in Canada.

Contents

Acknowledgments

Cover drawing: Columbus' ship, the **Santa María**
John Hollis-Hollis Associates

Cover photograph: The Snark, one of the first Air Force inter-
continental strategic missiles; it has now been made obsolete
by more powerful and accurate models.
United States Air Force

Page 2: Astronaut Edward H. White during his spectacular
"space walk" on June 3, 1965
National Aeronautics and Space Administration

Frontis: An American infantryman in Korea whose friend had
just been killed is comforted by another soldier
U.S. Army Photograph

Opposite: Portrait of Albert Einstein, twentieth-century scientist
whose theory of relativity opened the door to the Atomic Age
Historical Pictures Service, Chicago

Designer: John Hollis

Project Editor: Joan Downing

*Editorial Staff: Frances Dyra,
    Mary Reidy, Gerri Stoller*

THE MODERN WORLD

Introduction

There is no exact year, day, or hour in which the modern world began—the change from the Medieval World to the Modern World was gradual. For convenience, many historians use the year 1453 to mark the end of the Middle Ages. On this date Constantinople fell to the Turks, bringing to an end the Byzantine Empire.

After this event, historical emphasis shifts from eastern Europe to western Europe. In the West new *nation-states* —including France, England, and Spain—were to become centers for new developments. The East remained under Islamic influence, which produced a culture very different from that of the West.

In the West, just before the fall of Constantinople and continuing long after it, there came a period of intellectual reawakening that would produce countless new ideas and inventions. This revival influenced development in all areas of art, literature, religion, education, government, and science. The fifteenth-century modern man felt that he must think, experiment, discover, and use all the sources of knowledge available.

The span of modern history covers only about five hundred years. Yet within this short time much has changed. Change is perhaps the most outstanding characteristic of this period. The history of the modern world is in great part a record of the many developments and improvements that have completely altered everyday life. In this era, a new world was discovered. New governments were established. The middle class became more and more important. This new class struggled for changes in government and working conditions. In laboratories around the world new industrial practices and scientific discoveries took form. A new world was molded.

The Renaissance

Wars and the rise and fall of civilizations are important historical events. But more important than governments or rulers are the ideas and intellectual achievements that each generation has given to enrich our heritage.

A most outstanding historical period bridges the gap between the Medieval World and the Modern World. Beginning in the fourteenth century and continuing for several hundred years, this period produced many changes. Even before Constantinople fell in 1453 or the New World was discovered in 1492, men on the continent of Europe were paving the way for modern history. This period is called the *Renaissance* (ren' uh-sahnss), which means rebirth, or "born again." During this time men renewed their interest in the art and learning of classical times.

Not since the fall of the civilizations in Rome and Greece hundreds of years before, had men accomplished so much in art, literature, philosophy, and science. Every area of life was explored, examined, and reevaluated. Gradually men of learning in all walks of life began to study, question, and think about the world they lived in. Medieval minds had stressed the next world. Renaissance scholars thought mostly of this world—how to improve it, how to understand it, and how to enjoy and enrich it. These men have been called *humanists*. They truly lived up to their name, for they were concerned first with the rights and abilities of the individual and placed great importance on individual dignity and the worth of man.

The Renaissance began in Italy. In the wealthy Italian cities of Rome, Venice, Genoa, and Florence, the necessary ingredients for the renewal of learning were found. Unlike countries in the north and west, Italy had never lost contact with Constantinople and the Near East. From these cities, Mediterranean ideas and learning spread throughout the continent. When Constantinople fell to the Turks, forcing Byzantine scholars to seek refuge in Italy, many carried long-lost manuscripts with them, in addition to manuscripts written by Arab scholars.

Although interest in the classics (ancient Greek and Roman languages and culture) was characteristic of the

Renaissance, the writers of this period did much to further the popular use of their own languages. Most of them wrote great prose and poetry in their native tongue. Up to this time, most men had written in Latin, for much of the writing had been limited to religious subjects. This use of the vernacular (native languages) made it possible for the ideas of Renaissance writers to reach their own people. Most of the things written at this time reflect the society of the time—both the good and the bad. No one was free from criticism or examination—not even the church.

One of the first major Renaissance writers was Dante. His famous epic, *The Divine Comedy*, takes the reader on a make-believe trip to the "next world" in which Dante interviews famous people who were no longer living during his time. This great work both reflects Dante's society and criticizes it.

Humanism and the Renaissance spread to Germany, Holland, France, and England. Each of these countries had many towns and a thriving business life. This was a perfect climate for the renewal of learning. In agricultural areas and countries where feudalism was still strong this was not so. Thus, very little of this renewal reached Hungary, and Russia was untouched.

Writing, of course, was the first area of importance at the beginning of the Renaissance, for this made possible the spread of the new ideas. But other cultural areas soon were greatly influenced by these ideas. Art, especially, changed dramatically during the Renaissance. Men began to turn from the old to develop new ideas that came to typify this period. Artists and sculptors began to paint secular (nonreligious) subjects in natural settings. Paintings and sculptures of human bodies were lifelike, and artists learned how to paint with *perspective*—the difficult art of creating depth and distance in a flat painting.

Some of the great artists of this period were Michelangelo, Raphael, Rembrandt, Dürer, and da Vinci. Michelangelo was a painter, a sculptor, an architect, and a poet. He thought nothing of spending years working on any statue or painting that he was doing. Most people believe he was the greatest sculptor who ever lived. His statues of David, the boy who slew Goliath with his slingshot, and the

Michelangelo in His Studio, a painting by Eugène Delacroix

Hebrew prophet Moses are two of the most magnificent sculptures in the world. One of his most beautiful is called *The Pietá*, a sculpture of Mary holding her dying son Jesus in her lap.

Michelangelo lived to be nearly ninety years old, but because he could not stand being bored by people he usually had very little to do with them. He lived apart, almost totally involved in his work.

Raphael, another famous Italian artist, lived at the same time Michelangelo lived. Raphael, however, was just the opposite of Michelangelo in one way. Raphael loved company; he was very popular and constantly was surrounded by his many friends and admirers.

Raphael painted many beautiful Madonnas, which were pictures of the Virgin Mary with the infant Jesus. Madonnas were almost the only kind of pictures that artists painted then. Raphael painted one especially beautiful picture of Mary and Jesus called the *Sistine Madonna*. This is considered one of the greatest pictures in the world. It was painted for a small church, but was later placed in a great art gallery in Dresden, Germany.

Raphael died when he was still a young man, but he had worked so hard and so continuously that he left a large number of pictures.

Leonardo da Vinci is another great artist who lived at this time. He could be called a jack-of-all-trades, but unlike most jacks-of-all-trades, he was good at all the things he did. He was an artist, an engineer, a poet, and a scientist. It is said that he drew the first map of the New World that had the name "America" on it. He made very few paintings, because he did so many other things beside paint, but these few pictures are extremely beautiful. One, *The Last Supper*, is considered one of the greatest paintings in the world. Unfortunately, it was painted directly on a plastered wall, and in the course of time much of the plaster with the paint has peeled off, so that now there is little left of the original painting.

As we have said, this period called the Renaissance was characterized by a renewed interest in the affairs of this world, rather than the salvation of the soul in the next. Therefore, as you might expect, science became more and more important. Men sought to learn and understand more about the world they lived in. Aided especially by Arab and Greek writings, Renaissance scholars began to formulate and test new scientific ideas.

All these things were important beginnings, however, and laid the foundation for further developments and discoveries in the fields we have mentioned. The learning of the Renaissance was furthered and preserved by the universities that had begun to develop during the late Middle Ages. Many of these great institutions still exist today in Bologna, Paris, Oxford, and other European cities.

Age of Discovery—Columbus

Many people during the late Renaissance still believed the world was flat and that it was not safe for a ship to sail out of sight of land.

With renewed interest in the writings of the Greek and Roman scholars, however, more and more educated men began to reveal their theories regarding the physical world. One of the most important classical scholars was a Greek named Ptolemy (tahl' eh-mee), who wrote that the world was round. The earth, according to his theory, was the center of the universe, and around it traveled other planets, the sun, the moon, and the stars. Ptolemy also drew a map of the world. This map showed only the continents that were known then—eastern Europe, western Asia, and northern Africa. The western hemisphere was unknown in the second century. Thus his map placed the land mass of Europe close to that of Asia. This mistake made the distance between the continents seem shorter than it really was and could have been one of the reasons that Columbus would later sail westward with such a firm conviction that he would reach the Indies.

Although in the ninth and tenth centuries Norse seamen, led by Eric the Red and his son Leif, had reached new lands to the West, this fact does not seem to have been known by people of Europe during the Renaissance. Renaissance writings of the fifteenth century do not refer to these voyages and discoveries, though Scandinavian writings of the time do refer to them, and also to the settlement of Vinland, on the shores of the Atlantic Ocean. As time goes by, more and more evidence comes to light that seems to point

Bob Brunton—Hollis Associates

right: Galileo, the Renaissance scientist who proved that planets move around the sun rather than around the earth

opposite: Henry the Navigator

to the fact that the Norsemen reached the shores of North America long before the discovery of the New World by Christopher Columbus.

The desire for riches led seamen and kings to explore new areas. Ever since the eleventh century when the Crusaders had brought back the wondrous products of the East, interest in far-off lands had been aroused. After the fall of Constantinople, which had been a trading center for such products, the desire to find a safe route to the East increased. Printing had made Marco Polo's tales of his adventures and travels in strange lands a popular and frequently read book. All these things encouraged people to travel and trade with these lands.

Perhaps the most important products found in the East and sought after in the West were various spices. At this time there was no refrigeration and meat was often slightly spoiled before it reached the table. The creative use of spices hid the foul taste and increased the appetites of the diners.

If you look at the trade map you can see the trade routes most commonly used during this period. Most of the goods from India, Asia, China, and the Spice Islands were carried overland to seaports on the Mediterranean. Constantinople and Alexandria were in the hands of the Arabs. Other small ports were held by the Italian city-states. These Italian cities—particularly Genoa and Venice—enjoyed a large share of the profits from this trading. Goods passed through their ports and only later were shipped overland or by sea to cities in France, Spain, Portugal, England, Italy, and Germany.

Understandably, the businessmen in these countries did not like this set up, for most of the trade profits were going to the Italian cities. So they began to seek other ways to obtain their goods. First to take the lead in exploration was the tiny country of Portugal. This land is bordered by the Atlantic on one side and Spain on the other. In 1415, the Portuguese people had driven out the Mohammedans— called Moors in Portugal—and now were ruled by a king. In the mid-1400's their prince, named Henry, began a school for seamen. In his school he collected all the nautical information and equipment he could. He hired expert seamen to teach others all they knew about the seas and other lands. He used the latest equipment, such as the *compass* and the *astrolabe*. The magnetic needle of the compass showed direction. The astrolabe was an instrument that enabled men at sea to figure their position by measuring the position of the heavenly bodies in relation to the horizon. Unfortunately, this instrument was useful only when the weather was clear, but it was better than nothing.

This prince of Portugal is called Henry the Navigator because of his interest in the sea. He began sending his sea captains down the Atlantic coast of Africa. Each voyage took them farther in their explorations than had the one before. As they went they added to their knowledge of geography and made new maps. They also picked up ivory, gold, and slaves from their trade with the natives.

Finally, in 1488, a Portuguese sea captain named Bartholomeu Dias (dee'ahs) went so far south that he reached the tip of Africa. When he saw that the land he had been following was no longer to the east but now was to the west, he realized he was someplace new and unknown. Dias named the shore which was the tip of Africa the Cape of Storms because it was discovered during a storm. When he returned with this news to his king, however, it was renamed the Cape of Good Hope. Seamen knew now that ships could reach India by traveling around Africa.

Perhaps one of the most famous explorers was Christopher Columbus. He was born in 1451 in the city of Genoa, at the top of the Italian "boot." Like many other boys born in seaport towns, Columbus was very much interested in the sea. He had heard sailors tell tales of their travels. He had read the adventures of Marco Polo. He even knew about Ptolemy's belief that the world was round. So when his chance came he went to sea.

Like others of his times, Columbus longed to find a shorter route to the East. After much study and thought he became convinced that he could reach the Indies by sailing west. To the men of the fifteenth century the name "Indies" meant the lands of China, India, the East Indies, and Japan, where gold, gems, drugs, and spices were found.

Columbus knew the Portuguese were seeking a route around Africa. He thought this was the hard way to do it. Because he knew of the idea first developed by Ptolemy, Columbus believed the Indies were only about 3,000 miles west of Lisbon, Portugal. It would be easier to reach it this way than by going around Africa.

Columbus set out to prove that he was right. He went first to Portugal, but King John II refused to help him. His advisors told him that this Captain Columbus was wrong, the distance to the Indies was much greater. Thus they felt the idea wasn't practical and said it was better to continue explorations around Africa.

Disappointed, Columbus kept trying. He went to the court of Ferdinand and Isabella in Spain. At first the king and queen were too busy to really listen to his plan. They were fighting with the Mohammedans—called Moors in Spain as well as in Portugal—who had been in their country since 732. But in 1492, when the Spanish army drove the Moors out of their last stronghold, Granada, Ferdinand and Isabella were ready to consider his plan. The queen was much more interested in the adventure than was her husband. She was so interested she said she would sell her jewels to get money to finance this exploration to the West. This proved unnecessary, however, for the voyage was financed from the royal treasury. Three ships—the *Niña*, the *Pinta* and the *Santa María*—were equipped. These ships were vessels named *caravels*, made of wood and powered only by sails.

When Columbus was ready, he set sail from the port of Palos with a crew of about a hundred sailors. Directly toward the setting sun and into the vast reaches of the broad Atlantic Ocean Columbus steered. For weeks he kept sailing on and on. Columbus and his sailors were sailing toward the unknown. Never before had a ship been out of sight of land for so long a time. Even the Portuguese sailors kept close to the African coast. By the time the ships had been at sea for a month the sailors began to panic. It seemed impossible to them that any sea could be so vast or so endless, with absolutely nothing in sight. Their captain must be wrong. They must get him to turn back before it was too late. They began to beg the captain to turn back, saying there was nothing before them but more sea.

Columbus argued and argued, trying to convince his crews that they would reach land. Finally, on October 10, he promised to turn back if nothing were found in the next three days. Two days passed and nothing happened. Then at two o'clock on the morning of October 12, 1492, land was sighted. Columbus landed at Fernandez Bay on the island named San Salvador in the Bahamas. He lay claim to what was the New World and planted the flag of Spain in the sand. Their voyage of two months was a success. There *was* land in the West, just as Columbus had said. Because Columbus thought he had reached the islands of the Indies off the coast of Japan or China, he called the strange human beings he met there Indians.

Columbus explored the area hoping to discover the rich ports of China or Japan. He also hoped to present a letter he had to the emperor at Peking. But although he saw many villages and many natives he did not discover the cities he sought.

Today we know that Columbus sailed and explored the islands we know as the West Indies, so named because of his belief. These islands included Hispaniola, Puerto Rico, and Cuba.

Leaving a settlement on the island of Hispaniola, Columbus started for home on the *Niña*, sailing on January 16, 1493. He had found no gold or precious stones nor any of the other wonders of the East described by Marco Polo and

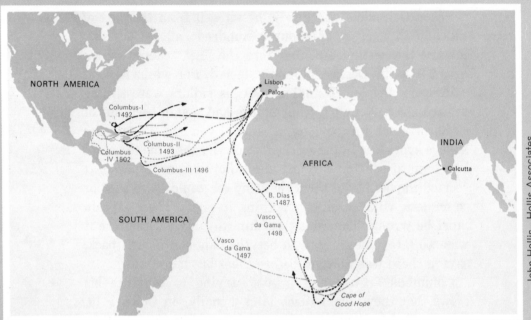

above: The explorations of Christopher Columbus

opposite: Columbus' ship, the *Santa María*

others. But he had found land. Taking several Indians with him to show to the people at home, and some tobacco—the first ever seen by Europeans—Columbus sailed for home.

The return voyage was very difficult. The *Santa María* was abandoned after being shipwrecked in Hispaniola and only the two smaller ships returned home. During an Atlantic storm the *Niña* and the *Pinta* were separated and blown off course. But they struggled on heroically, finally reaching the Azores (ah-zohrz'), islands in the north Atlantic belonging to Portugal. Here the authorities took Columbus in custody until he was able to convince them that he did not intend to trespass on Portuguese land in Africa. After being released, the *Niña* and the *Pinta* set sail for Spain, which they reached on March 15, 1493, landing at Palos.

Columbus rode across Spain and reported to the king and queen at their court in Barcelona. During the grand reception in his honor they bestowed on him the title Admiral of the Ocean Sea and Viceroy of the Indies; they also granted permission and royal support for him to organize a second expedition to the East.

The second fleet was larger and better equipped than the first had been. Reaching the new land, Columbus discovered that the Indians had killed all the men in the settlement on the island of Hispaniola. Columbus then brought his colonists to another part of Hispaniola where he set up a town called Isabella. This small beginning marked the first permanent European settlement in the western hemisphere.

In 1494 Columbus explored the islands of Cuba and Jamaica. When he returned home the Spaniards were saying that his discoveries weren't really so wonderful. There wasn't enough gold. None of the expected riches were found in this land. Still, the crown allowed a third voyage. This time Columbus searched for lands where gold and other precious goods could be found. He sailed along the coast of Venezuela. Stepping ashore, Columbus realized that he had found land unknown until then. He called it the "New World." But there was trouble. At home the people were making fun of his discoveries. In the new colonies he was trying to establish the people fought with each other. Finally, in 1500, a man was sent to Santo Domingo, the capital of Hispaniola, to settle the troubles. He captured

Columbus and his two brothers and transported them back to Spain in chains. Although he was promptly set free, Columbus was humiliated and he kept those chains as a perpetual reminder of man's ingratitude.

By 1501 the Spanish people were very disgusted with Columbus because he had not found riches and great wealth. But in 1502 he made another voyage. This time he was looking for a passage by sea between the island of Cuba and the continent of the New World. Columbus thought this passage would lead to China, for he believed that South America lay only a short distance from China's mainland. This idea held until 1522. The small fleet sailed up and down the coast of Central America looking for a waterway that wasn't there. They traded cloth and beads with the Indians of present-day Costa Rica and Panama; in return they received copper and gold objects such as masks and ornaments. The expedition ended in 1504 and all those that were left returned to Spain.

By this time Columbus' supporter, Isabella, had died. King Ferdinand would not listen to his report. Nor would he finance another expedition. Columbus was now fifty-three years old. He was poor and ill. The country he had done so much for refused to grant him either the titles or the money he deserved. Finally, in a humble home at Valladolid, Columbus died. His remains were sent to Santo Domingo for burial.

These were the adventures of one of the greatest discoverers of all times. Nothing ever stopped him from his quest. He began something that others would continue. He gave new ideas to others and discovered a continent that in itself would change the course of history.

A favorite story is told about how Columbus once answered those who were trying to belittle his achievements. During a dinner at the king's court, several nobles began to say his discovery wasn't so important. So Columbus passed an egg around the table, asking each noble if he could stand it on end. Each tried but no one could. When it came back to Columbus, he set it down just hard enough to crack the end slightly and flatten it. *Then*, of course, it stood on end. For as Columbus pointed out, it was very easy to do *if* you knew how. It was not hard for people to say how easy it was to sail west until land was found, for Columbus had done it and had shown the way.

Explorers and Explorations

When Columbus touched land in South America, he called it the "New World." For many years it was called by this name. But as knowledge and map making increased, names began to be given to certain sections. What should this new world be called? Today we might say that it should have been named after Columbus. But it wasn't, and this is why.

In 1497, an Italian named Amerigo Vespucci (vespoo'chee) came with an expedition to the southern part of the New World. When he returned home he wrote letters claiming to have discovered a new continent. These letters telling of his adventures and discovery were widely published. Then in 1507 the name America was used for the "New World" to honor the discoverer. Although we know now that it wasn't really Amerigo who discovered America, the name stuck.

While Columbus was trying to find the passage to the Indies along the coast of Central America, the Portuguese were continuing their explorations down the coast of Africa. Each year they went farther. Then in 1497, Vasco da Gama left Portugal. He followed Dias' route around the Cape of Good Hope and sailed to India where he docked in the city of Calcutta on May 20, 1498. Da Gama was the first man to find a sea route to the riches of India; he returned home with the spices and riches that Columbus sought in the West. Da Gama was praised and rewarded. A new trade route was born and from it Portugal began to prosper.

Still other explorers followed the lead of Columbus. They began to sail to the New World in the West. In 1498, an Italian named John Cabot, sailing under the flag of the king of England, discovered land he called Newfoundland. This discovery gave England a claim to part of the New World.

In 1500 a Portuguese named Cabral (kuh-brahl') set out to follow da Gama's route to the East. Cabral was caught in a storm and blown off course so that he ended up not off the coast of Africa but off the coast of South America. The section where he landed is now known as Brazil. After Cabral claimed the land for his king, he turned around and sailed back to India.

During this time the kings were strengthening their power and seeking new wealth. They wanted riches from their new territories. Needless to say, the rights of the natives, or "Indians," were not considered in this seizure of power.

24

Each voyage after Columbus led to increased knowledge of geography. In 1513, a Spanish explorer named Balboa (bal-boh' uh) sailed to Central America. Landing where Panama now is, Balboa crossed the land until finally he stood on a hill and viewed the Pacific Ocean. He called it the South Sea because it was facing the south.

Another important explorer later startled the world. He was Ferdinand Magellan, who sailed west from Spain across the Atlantic Ocean and reached the southern end of South America. Here he discovered a narrow waterway called a *strait*, now called the Strait of Magellan. Despite the twisting, churning seas he and his ships passed through the strait and entered a vast ocean. Magellan named this the "Pacific," which means calm, or peaceful, because after all the storms they had been through it seemed very calm and quiet.

The exploring ships sailed before the wind and reached the Philippine Islands. Here Magellan was killed, but the lands were claimed for Spain.

Three years after the expedition had set out in 1522 the survivors returned. Only one ship, the *Victoria*, was left and only eighteen men had survived to tell of their adventure.

This voyage proved several things to the world: The world was round. Asia could be reached by sailing west; but ships had to cross the Atlantic, pass through the Strait of Magellan, and go into the Pacific Ocean. The distance across the Pacific was greater than that across the Atlantic.

Yet men continued to look for a passage to the East. In 1524, Verrazano, an Italian, sailed along the coast of North America looking for a northwest passage, but he failed. He did, however, discover New York Harbor and the Hudson River. Today the longest suspension bridge in the world is named after him. Later Jacques Cartier (zhahk kahr-tyay) of France sailed up the St. Lawrence River hoping it would lead to the Pacific, but he was wrong. In 1610, Hendrik Hudson of Holland sought a northwest passage. He followed the broad Hudson River, but he failed to find the passage. In fact, not until almost four hundred years later would the only existing passage, through the Arctic Ocean, be found in the North. The voyages of Hudson and Cartier were the bases for Dutch and French claims to territory in the New World.

Spanish explorer Ferdinand Magellan sailed around the southern tip of South America and discovered a strait now called the Strait of Magellan

The Search for Gold and Adventure

Most of the early explorers did not stay very long in the new lands, but others soon began to map and explore the interiors. They discovered or invented the wealth and wonder of this New World—from legendary cities of gold to the fountain of eternal youth.

Men of daring and adventure went to the New World. One was a Spaniard named Ponce de Leon (pawn' thay day lay-awn'), who conquered Puerto Rico in 1508. Hearing Indian tales that told of an island named Bimini that supposedly contained a fountain of youth, Ponce de Leon went in search of such a place. In seeking Bimini, he found Florida in 1513. He claimed it for the Spanish on Easter Sunday. Ponce de Leon died after an unsuccessful attempt to set up a colony in 1521.

Another daring explorer was Hernando de Soto (dee soh'toh), who searched for El Dorado, the city supposedly built of solid gold. While searching for El Dorado, de Soto discovered and crossed the longest river in America—the Mississippi. In 1539, he landed with 600 men, on the coast of Florida. In his search he passed through the southeastern United States. But instead of finding El Dorado, de Soto was taken sick with a fever and died. The Spaniards, to make the Indians fear them, had said that de Soto was a god and could not die. So, in order to cover up the fact that de Soto had died, his men buried him at night in the river he had discovered. They then told the Indians that he had gone on a trip to heaven and would return presently.

The central part of America at this time was called Mexico. A tribe of Indians known as Aztecs lived there. These Aztecs were highly civilized. They lived in lovely houses, and built fine temples and palaces. They made roads and aqueducts something like those of the Romans, and had enormous treasures of silver and gold. And yet the Aztecs worshipped idols and sacrificed human beings to them. Their king was a famous warrior named Montezuma.

A Spaniard named Cortez was sent to conquer the Aztecs. He landed on the shore of Mexico early in 1519 with 650 men and 16 horses. Cortez burned his ships so that his sailors and soldiers could not turn back. The Aztecs thought these white-faced people were gods who had come down from heaven and that their ships with their white sails were white-winged birds that had borne them to earth. They had never seen horses, and they were astonished at what seemed to them terrible beasts that the white men

above: Cortez and his men in Mexico with the Aztec chief, Montezuma

below: Exploration routes of the fifteenth and sixteenth centuries

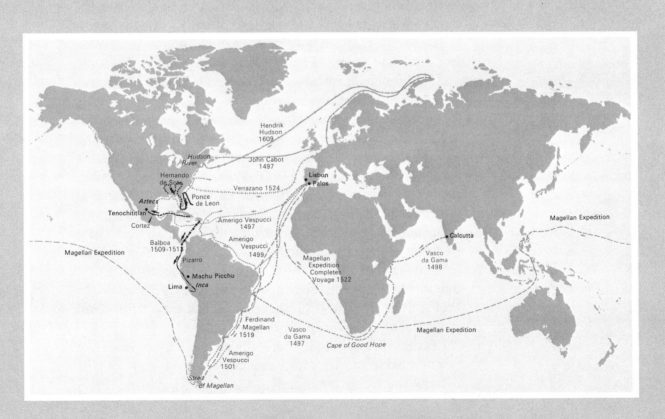

rode. When the Spaniards fired their cannon, the Aztecs were terrified. They thought it was thunder and lightning.

Cortez moved on toward the Aztec capital, called Tenochtitlán, now Mexico City, which was built on an island in the middle of a lake. The natives he met on the way fought desperately, but as they had only weapons such as men used in the Stone and Bronze Ages, they were no match against the guns and cannon of the Spaniards.

Montezuma, their chief, wishing to make friends with these white gods, sent Cortez cartloads of gold. When Cortez reached the capital city, Montezuma treated him as a guest instead of an enemy and entertained him royally. Then suddenly Cortez took Montezuma prisoner and used him as a hostage so he himself could rule the people. The Aztecs were very angry and soon terrible fighting began. The Aztecs fought desperately and bravely, but the Spanish guns were too much for them. Cortez defeated the Indians on the Plain of Otumba on July 7, 1520. He claimed the rich land and called it New Spain.

In Peru in South America was another tribe of civilized Indians who were even wealthier than the Aztecs. They were called Incas, and it was said that in their cities the streets were paved with gold. Another Spaniard named Pizarro (pih-zahr' oh) went to Peru to conquer the Incas as Cortez had conquered the Aztecs in Mexico.

After much hardship, Pizarro—with orders from the king of Spain to conquer the people—arrived in Peru. He found conditions just right for conquest. The ruler, called Atahualpa, had taken the throne from his brother but had not yet defeated all his enemies. Pizarro took Atahualpa prisoner. Bargaining for his freedom, Atahualpa promised Pizarro enough gold and silver to fill two huge rooms. But after receiving the treasure, Pizarro strangled his victim.

Organizing a Spanish government, Pizarro ruled Peru. He founded the city of Lima, now the capital. Many of the defeated Indians fled to the mountains and built new cities. One of these, Machu Picchu, was not discovered until the 1950's. It is very well preserved and has taught us much about the ancient Incan civilization.

France, Holland, and England also sent out explorers to conquer parts of America, and missionaries to teach the Indians the Christian religion.

Religious Reform

Since the fall of Rome in 476, Christianity had spread and the authority of the church in the West was at a high point. Since he controlled most of central and northern Italy, the pope was in fact a king. He was at the same time supposedly the spiritual leader of all Christians—kings and serfs alike.

As the Dark Ages passed, the leaders in the countries of western Europe began to believe the pope had too much power. They resented the fact that the church held huge grants of land given under the feudal system and in addition received all the money given by the faithful. When kings were looking for money, it seemed to them that all the money was going to Rome. Also the pope sometimes used his authority over people to force a political decision. This made the kings angry. They felt that all political authority belonged to them and to no one else.

During and after the Hundred Years' War, the people began to feel more loyalty to their kings than ever before. The rise of towns and the increase in trade encouraged business and finance. Yet traditional church ideas were opposed to profits and interest. The new learning opened men's minds and they began to question some of the teachings of the church. Heresy—which was a term used for all religious teachings, ideas, and practices that were different from those of Rome—began to be considered by Christian thinkers in an intellectual way rather than an emotional one. People became more independent, for the Renaissance had encouraged men to think for themselves.

But perhaps the most important reason for the growing disenchantment with the church was the outward behavior of the church and her clergy. Wealthy people could buy high church offices for their sons or other relatives. Many members of the clergy lived wicked lives, practicing none of their vows. Through their sinful lives they were a bad example and people began to criticize the church and its bad leaders in books and speeches.

This, then, was the condition of the Roman Catholic Church early in the 1500's. And this is how the Reformation began.

Pope Leo X at this time was building a great church in Rome. This church was to be called St. Peter's, and was to take the place of the old church that Constantine had built on the spot where St. Peter was supposed to have been crucified. The Pope wanted it to be the largest and finest church in the world.

St. Peter's was to be the capitol of the Christian religion. But besides all this, the pope needed an enormous amount of money to build this magnificent church. He had to get the money from the people. Like other popes had done, he offered *indulgences* for sale. According to the teachings of the Roman Catholic church, a man could win pardon from some of the penalty of a misdeed or sin with an indulgence, if—and this is the most important part—he was really sorry for his error. Unfortunately, at this time people often bought indulgences without being penitent. This practice of buying and selling indulgences was much abused.

The pope opened the sale of indulgences to raise funds for St. Peter's in Rome. In Germany the archbishop who supposedly represented the pope began to offer them to the German people. To promote a good sale he hired a priest named Tetzel, who was a "supersalesman." This man went around to different churches selling his indulgences. To make a good sales record, Tetzel began telling the people that indulgences would pardon them from not only past sins but future ones, too. He never mentioned that they had to be truly sorry for a sin to have an indulgence be of any help. Tetzel was wrong, but no one stopped him.

Finally, an Augustinian monk named Martin Luther who lived and taught at the University of Wittenberg, protested against Tetzel's preaching and selling. Martin Luther thought that not only this, but also many other things in the Catholic church were not right. So, on October 31, 1517, he made a list of ninety-five things he thought were not right and nailed it up on the church door at Wittenberg. This door was like a town bulletin board. This act caused a great stir. Some people agreed with Luther. Some disagreed.

The arguments went on and on. Finally Luther had a debate with a representative of the pope, a man named Johann Eck. Going away from the question of indulgences,

Eck asked Luther not what his beliefs were, but whether he would submit to the authority of his superiors—the pope or the church council. In answer to this, Luther made a positive statement of personal freedom. He declared, "I cannot and I will not recant (take back) anything, for to go against conscience is neither right nor safe."

Now a rebel, Luther was forced to leave the church. He was *excommunicated*. But this was no longer the medieval world with its blind obedience to the church. Now many people who agreed with Luther left the Roman Catholic church when he was excommunicated.

The pope called on the king of Spain, Charles V, to help in this quarrel with Luther. He called him for aid because he was not only a good church member, but because as king of the Holy Roman Empire he was the most powerful ruler in Europe.

Charles commanded Luther to come to a city named Worms (vohrmz) to be tried. He promised Luther that no harm would come to him, and so Luther went. When Luther arrived at Worms, Charles ordered him to take back all he had said. Luther refused. Some of Charles' nobles said Luther should be burned at the stake. But Charles, as he had promised, let him go and did not punish him for his belief. Luther's friends, however, were afraid that other members of the church might do him harm. They knew Luther would not take care of himself, so they themselves took him prisoner and kept him shut up for over a year so no one could harm him. While Luther was in prison he translated the Bible into German. This was the first time the Bible had been written in that language. Luther also began to outline formally the beliefs of his new religion, which was based on salvation by faith alone and private interpretation of the Bible.

In 1529 Charles again considered the new belief. He called together a court, a *Diet*, and formally declared Lutheranism a heresy and Luther a heretic. But many of the German people still would not accept this judgment. They *protested*, so they were called *Protestants*. Even today those Western Christians who are not Roman Catholics are still called Protestants.

Today in most countries people of different religions live side by side in peace, each allowing the other his right to choose a belief. But in the sixteenth century this was not so. Catholics were deadly enemies of Protestants. Each side was sure that it alone was right and that the other side was

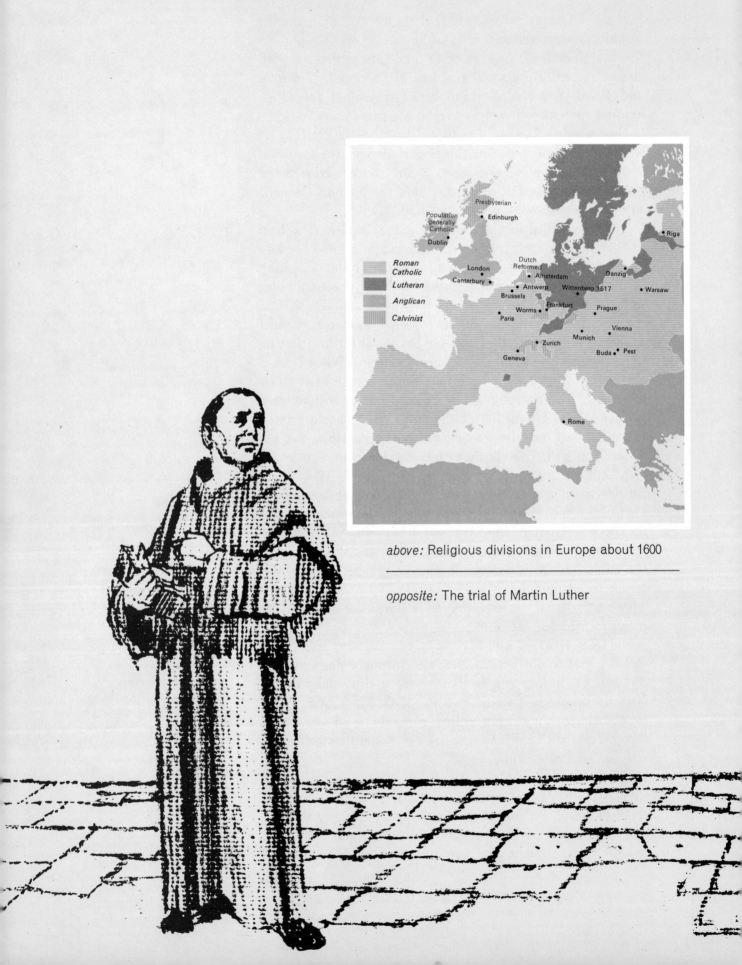

above: Religious divisions in Europe about 1600

opposite: The trial of Martin Luther

Within the map:

Presbyterian

Population
generally
Catholic

Edinburgh

Riga

Roman
Catholic

Lutheran

Anglican

Calvinist

Dublin

London
Canterbury

Dutch
Reformed

Amsterdam

Antwerp
Brussels

Wittenberg 1517

Danzig

Warsaw

Worms
Frankfurt

Prague

Paris

Vienna

Zurich

Munich

Geneva

Buda Pest

Rome

wrong. They fought each other furiously and bitterly. Friends and relatives murdered each other because they thought differently about religion—and yet all called themselves Christians. It was a religious civil war.

Fighting broke out first in Germany. For twenty-five years each side fought the other. Neither side was victorious, but in 1555 the Peace of Augsburg was signed. This peace said that each prince could decide what religion would be followed in his state. Church lands taken over by the states before 1552 remained part of the states. The peace also said that the only Protestant group to be allowed in Germany would be Lutherans—thus, there was no real religious freedom. Lutherans in Catholic states were to be allowed to follow their consciences, as would Catholics in Lutheran states.

People in the north of Germany believed in Lutheranism, while those in the south chose Catholicism. Even today this religious difference exists, although all religions are at peace.

During this time, new religious ideas were developing in other lands also. By 1527, the kings of Norway and Denmark recognized both the Catholic and Lutheran religions, but after a Catholic rebellion was stopped, both lands made Lutheranism the state religion. Soon Sweden followed suit —naming Lutheranism the state religion.

In Switzerland John Calvin became the founder of another belief. Soon all of Switzerland followed Calvinism. From here, ideas spread to Catholic France. As had happened in Germany, religious differences brought war and death in France. This religious warring was finally brought to an end in 1598 by a decree— the Edict of Nantes—which accepted the religious and political rights of the Calvinists, or Huguenots as they were called in France.

In the Netherlands the people split. The southern group chose Catholicism. This area is now southern Belgium and its people are called Walloons. The Flemish people of Holland and northern Belgium chose Calvinism.

In Scotland, under the leadership of John Knox, the Calvinist Presbyterian church overcame the Catholic authorities.

Some of the new thinking reached England, but her king, Henry VIII, strongly resisted it. Henry's last name was Tudor. So many kings had first names that were alike that such names were numbered to tell which Charles or Henry was meant and how many of the same name there had been before. Henry VIII was at first a strong Catholic, and once wrote a book on religion for which the pope had given him the title "Defender of the Faith."

But Henry wanted a strong kingdom. And he had a wife Catherine, daughter of the king of Spain, whom he wanted to get rid of because she had borne him no son. Henry wanted a son to inherit his kingdom. In order to get rid of Catherine so that he might marry again, he had to set his marriage aside—obtain a divorce. Henry asked the pope to arrange this because the pope at Rome, as head of the Catholic church, was the only one who could dissolve the marriage. The pope refused to do so. He would not allow Henry to set aside his wife and marriage.

Henry knew what he wanted. He himself was ruler, and he did not intend to let any foreign pope in Rome stop him. Henry himself divorced his wife through a religious court of his own choosing. Thus he broke with the church. Then in 1534 Henry passed a law called the Act of Supremacy which declared that henceforth Henry and all his heirs would be head of all the Christians in England.

After Catherine, Henry VIII had five wives, six in all; not all at one time, of course, for Christians could have only one wife at a time. His first wife he divorced, the second he beheaded, the third died. The same thing happened to his last three wives; the first he divorced, the second he beheaded, and the third died—but Henry died before she did.

That was how religious reform, the *Reformation*, swept across Europe. The Roman Catholic church had been the main force uniting the old Holy Roman Empire. With the Reformation, many kings and princes broke with Rome and made some form of Protestantism the official religion of the countries they ruled. People became more aware of the differences between themselves and people from other lands. When the people of a country think of themselves as a group rather than as individuals, we call this *nationalism*. Thus, where before the Reformation everyone in western Europe was more or less a Catholic and a subject of the Holy Roman Emperor, there now were French Catholics, German Lutherans, Swiss Calvinists, and the Anglican Church in England. The rise of nationalism was to change forever the map and history of Europe.

British Information Services

King Henry VIII of England

England Gains Control of the Sea

Henry's son, Edward VI, became king, for although he was younger than his sisters, a boy was supposed to be more fit to rule than a girl. But Edward didn't live long and Mary, daughter of Henry and Catherine of Aragon became queen. She was married to Philip II, king of Spain and ruler of the Netherlands, Portugal, and Spanish America.

Mary did not approve of what her father had done when he turned against the pope and the Catholic church. Mary herself was a devout Catholic and ready to fight for the pope and the Catholic church. When she became queen she did several things. First she made Parliament take back the laws that declared England to be Protestant. Then she began to force people back into the Catholic church. If Protestants didn't return, they were put to death. During her reign of five years, England—like France and Germany— had many religious persecutions. For her part in this religious war, the queen came to be called Bloody Mary.

Mary's husband Philip was even more intolerant than Mary about religion at home. Philip tried to force all those who were not Catholic—even Jews and Moslems who were not even Christians—to become Catholic.

People of this time believed their rulers had the right, in fact the duty, to punish those whose religious beliefs differed from the king's. In Italy, and especially in Spain, special religious courts were set up. These courts were called the Holy Office, or *Inquisition*. Those suspected of being heretics, or Protestants, or non-Christians, were tormented in all sorts of horrible ways. They were given the choice of either submitting to the church and doing penance or being burned alive at the stake. Sentences were carried out by government officials on the orders of the Catholic church.

Philip had great plans for himself and for Spain. He wanted to unite Spain under the rule of a powerful king. He also wanted to make his land strong and wealthy. So he began to force people to do what he wanted them to do.

Naturally many people didn't like this. They began to fight back. They *revolted*.

The people of the Netherlands were led by a man called William the Silent. In 1581 they drew up a paper which has been called the Dutch Declaration of Independence. They pledged to fight for their freedom. Surprisingly successful against their powerful enemy, Spain, the Dutch were able to prevent a Spanish victory on land by flooding it to stop advancing armies. On sea they did very well also. The Dutch fleet attacked Spanish ships and raided the colonies.

Even after William the Silent was killed by order of King Philip, the war dragged on and wasn't settled until about a hundred and ten years later!

The Dutch people were aided in fighting the Spanish armies by one of Philip's rivals for power. This was the ruler of England, Elizabeth I, one of history's greatest queens.

Elizabeth was the daughter of Henry VIII and Anne Boleyn. She had inherited the throne when her sister, Mary —the wife of Philip of Spain—had died. A tall, slender woman, this queen ruled from 1558 until 1603.

Because she was the daughter of Henry's second wife, members of the Catholic faith did not believe Elizabeth had the right to inherit the throne. They felt that Henry's second marriage was invalid. But Elizabeth was determined to be queen, so she decided to support the Church of England. During her reign, the Church of England became the official national religion. Elizabeth felt that those who did not support the Church of England also did not support the English monarchy. Her religious persecutions of Catholics and others therefore tended to be political in tone, rather than religious, though of course the end result in death or torture was the same.

Perhaps one of the most dramatic executions in history took place during Elizabeth's reign. This was the beheading of the beautiful queen of Scotland, Mary Stuart. This Catholic queen had a claim to the throne of England because she was descended from an English king. She had troubles at home, however. Her country, Scotland, had become Protestant. The people were not happy being ruled by a Catholic. Also, Mary Stuart became involved in several plots against the people. Finally, after she was accused of murder, she fled to England. Here she was given protection for a time. As she was next in line for the throne after Elizabeth, however, and a Catholic, she soon became involved in plots formed by those who opposed Elizabeth. It soon became clear to Elizabeth that the plots, or the danger of such plots, would not end until Mary, queen of Scotland, was dead. She was beheaded on February 8, 1587. The execution of Mary upset the Catholic rulers of Europe, especially Philip II of Spain. He was determined to get rid of Elizabeth and to stop her ships from attacking his ships and giving his enemies financial aid. So Philip built a navy of over one hundred vessels. This fleet of warships was called the *Spanish Armada*. It was made up mostly of gal-

Marble bust of Philip II of Spain

Portrait of Queen Elizabeth I of England

leons which were large and awkward. Spain was proud of this fine fleet. Spaniards boastfully called it the "Invincible Armada" and believed it to be unbeatable.

The "Invincible Armada" set forth in 1588 to conquer England. Lined up in the shape of a half-moon, the ships sailed grandly toward England.

The English fleet was composed of smaller ships, and instead of going out to meet the Armada in regular sea battle as the Spaniards expected, the English ships sailed out and attacked the Spanish ships from behind. They fought one ship at a time. The English were better gunners than the Spanish, and their smaller boats were faster and easier to manage. The English could strike and get away before a Spanish ship could turn around into firing position. So gradually the English sank or destroyed the big Spanish boats, one by one.

Then the English set afire some old ships and let them drift into the Spanish fleet. Since all boats at that time were made of wood, the Spaniards became frightened at these burning wrecks drifting down upon them, and part of the fleet quickly went the other way. The rest tried to get back to Spain by sailing north of Scotland. But a terrible storm struck, and most of the ships were wrecked. Thousands of dead bodies were washed up on shore. Thus the great Spanish Armada was destroyed, and with it ended Spanish sea power. Spain was never again the great nation she had been.

Illustration shows the Spanish fleet they called the "Invincible Armada"

Expansion of England

Queen Elizabeth I never married, so she had no children to rule after her. She was the last of the Tudor family, so the English had to look around for a new ruler. In those days Scotland was a separate country and not part of England as it is now. James Stuart, the son of Mary Stuart, was then king of Scotland. The English invited him to come and rule over them because he was related to the Tudors. He accepted the invitation and became James I of England.

A body of men called Parliament was supposed to make the laws for the English people. But James said that Parliament could do nothing that he didn't like, and if they weren't very careful he wouldn't let them do any governing at all. James said that whatever the king did was right, that the king could do no wrong, that God gave kings the right to do as they pleased with their subjects. This was called the *divine right of kings*. Naturally, the English people would not put up with this sort of thing. Ever since King John signed the Magna Carta in 1215, they had insisted on their own rights. Quarrels started, of course, but the real fight came with the next king and not with James.

Nothing much happened in England itself during James's reign, but in other countries a great deal did happen, although the king had little to do with it. English people made settlements in India and in America, and these grew until at last India, and part of America also, belonged to England.

One settlement in America was made in the south, and one was made in the north. Raleigh's settlement at Roanoke disappeared, but in 1607, a boatload of English gentlemen sailed over to America looking for adventure and gold. They arrived in Virginia and named the place where they settled Jamestown after their king. They found no gold, and they didn't want to work. But their leader, Captain John Smith, took matters in hand and said that those who didn't work wouldn't eat, so the colonists worked.

A little later another company of people left England for America. These people were not looking for riches as the Jamestown settlers had been; they were looking for a place where they might worship God as they pleased. This company of people left England in 1620 in a ship called the *Mayflower*, sailed across the ocean, and landed at a place called Plymouth, in Massachusetts, where they set up a colony. More than half of them died during the first winter from hardship and exposure in the bitter northern weather, but they valued the freedom they found in America so highly that none of those who were left would go back to England. This settlement was the first in that part of the United States called New England.

below: English settlers landing at Plymouth, Massachusetts.
Their ship, the *Mayflower,* is anchored in the harbor.

Revolution and Reform in England

Charles I was the son of King James, and like his father he believed in the divine right of kings—that he alone had the right to say what should be done or what should not be done. He treated the English people as King John had treated them—as if they were there simply to suit his pleasure and to do as he wished.

England's people, however, loved liberty. They wanted Parliament to make their laws and do what was best for them whether the king liked it or not. But every time the king called Parliament together, a fight occurred. Charles would become angry and order Parliament to go home if they wouldn't agree with him.

In 1642, the king assembled an army of lords and nobles and those common people who agreed to fight for him. Those who took his side even dressed differently from those who were against him. They grew their hair in long curls, wore broad-brimmed hats with large feathers, lace collars, and had cuffs of lace even on their breeches.

These men were called *cavaliers*. Most of them were nobles, clergy, or country gentlemen. They stood for the established Church of England and the king.

Parliament also got together an army of the people who wanted their rights. They cut their hair short and wore hats with tall crowns and very simple clothes. They were called *roundheads*, and were mostly townspeople of the middle class. They stood for Parliament and the other Protestant churches.

The king's army won the first battles until a country gentleman named Oliver Cromwell trained a regiment of horse soldiers or cavalry to be such good fighters that they began to win. These men were known as "Ironsides."

At last, after three years of fighting, the king's army was beaten. King Charles fled to Scotland but his Scottish subjects captured him and turned him over to Cromwell and Parliament. The victorious Parliament could not decide what to do with the king. Then a small part of Parliament led by Cromwell took matters in their own hands, and though they had no right to do so, they tried King Charles for treason and condemned him to death. On January 30, 1649, Charles Stuart—king of England, Scotland, Ireland,

and Wales was beheaded.

England was now called a Commonwealth and was ruled by Parliament. But the people couldn't agree on how to run things. Finally, after years of trouble, Oliver Cromwell, the commander of the parliamentary army, took over. He dissolved Parliament and as military dictator ruled England for four years.

Cromwell was a coarse-looking person with rough manners, but he was honest and religious. He ruled England as a stern and strict father might rule his family—he would stand for no nonsense.

Cromwell was really a king although he called himself Lord Protector. But he did a great deal that was good for England. He built up the English Navy and beat the Dutch and Spanish on the sea. He gave real freedom to many Protestant groups and to Jews who had always been persecuted.

The rule of Britain by Cromwell had been strict. The English people were forbidden by law to dance, play cards, go to the theater, wear fancy clothes, and many other things. The English were so happy to be rid of rules that they forgot about their troubles under the Stuarts. So, in 1660, when the English found themselves without a ruler, they invited the son of Charles I, the king they had beheaded, to reign over them. Once more a Stuart—Charles II—became king.

above left: The Great Fire of London, 1666

above: Portrait of Charles I of England

Charles was called the Merry Monarch because all he seemed to think about was eating and drinking, amusing himself, and having a good time. He made fun of things that were holy and sacred.

During his reign an old and terrible disease, the plague, broke loose again in London. Some people thought that God had caused it; that he was shocked by the behavior of the king and his people—especially their behavior toward holy things. They thought God was punishing them. The next year, 1666, a great fire started in London. Thousands of houses and hundreds of churches were destroyed. But the Great Fire, as it was called, cleaned up the disease and dirt and therefore was really a blessing. London had been a city of wooden houses. It was rebuilt of brick and stone.

When Charles II died, his brother became King James II. A Catholic, James openly tried to restore Catholicism and the absolute power of the king. The English didn't want either. When James' son was born, the English felt that the threat to their liberty was doubled and threatened to rebel again. James finally abdicated his throne and fled to France in 1688.

Once again England was without a ruler. Parliament asked James' eldest daughter, Mary, to rule. She was married to William of Orange, the ruler of the Netherlands. Before they were crowned they had to agree to do what Parliament wanted them to do. A law was passed saying that the ruler of England must belong to the Church of England. In addition, in 1688, Parliament drew up an agreement called the Bill of Rights, which William and Mary signed. This agreement made Parliament ruler over the nation, and ever since Parliament, and not the king, has been the real ruler of England.

The declaration settled the difficulties between the king and Parliament. It said that the king was an official chosen by Parliament and subject to its laws. Without the approval of Parliament, the king could not pass tax laws, or support an army or navy. Members of Parliament would be elected. The right to freedom of speech and fair and just trials were also given to the people. When a later act allowed freedom of religion—with only some restrictions on certain groups—England was on the way to becoming a free and democratic nation.

Rise of the French Monarchy

Across the English Channel another nation-state was beginning to grow—the ancient land of Gaul, now called France. We shall see how this country developed and strengthened its monarchy. This development was very different from England's for in France the king ruled absolutely—that is he had no one to check his power. His word was law.

When he was sixteen Louis XIII of the Bourbon family took over the throne of France. Unlike his father, Louis wasn't a strong ruler, but he was smart enough to pick a good man to help him. This man was not a noble or a general but a cardinal. Cardinals are church officials who are just below the pope. They are called "Princes of the Church" and as marks of their office they wear a red cap and gown. The cardinal picked by Louis was named Richelieu (rish' uh-lyoo). He ruled France "behind the scenes" from 1624 to 1642. Richelieu wanted to do two things in France—two things that would be very difficult for him to accomplish. First, he wanted to make the king's authority supreme in France, and second, he wanted to make France the greatest nation on the European continent.

The last great religious conflict between Protestants and Catholics was fought during Richelieu's ministry. It began in 1618 and lasted until 1648. It was called the Thirty Years' War. This war was to give Richelieu the chance to win for the Bourbon family power and land from a rival family—the Hapsburgs. The Hapsburg family had ruled many German states as Holy Roman Emperors since the fifteenth century.

The war began with a dispute between Protestant and Catholic German citizens in Bohemia. Fighting broke out and the Catholic king of Bohemia—Ferdinand, of the Hapsburg family—was thrown out and a Protestant ruler was put in his place. Not long after being ousted from his throne, Ferdinand was elected Emperor of the Holy Roman Empire. This empire was a loose combination of states throughout Europe that pledged support to their elected leader. As emperor of an area that included many of the small German states, Ferdinand got together a large army and returned to Bohemia. His army was successful in defeating the Protestant forces—Bohemia was conquered and brought under the Hapsburg's control. But the fight had just begun.

The religious cause was later taken up by Protestant Denmark and Sweden. Denmark was soon defeated in battle and retired from the scene. Sweden, however, continued to fight. Led by their great general-king, Gustavus Adolphus, the well-trained, well-equipped Swedish army came to the aid of the fighting Protestant German states. Their military successes in 1631 and 1632 strengthened the hope of the Protestant states that they would be able to defeat the powerful Hapsburg army. Gustavus Adolphus was killed in battle, however, and no other Swedish general was able to carry on with his military success. The fighting and killing went on and on.

In 1635, Cardinal Richelieu stepped in to side with the Protestants against the Hapsburgs. In doing so he hoped to gain territory for France and thereby make his nation stronger. He also hoped to weaken the power of the Hapsburgs—France's great rival on the continent.

This completely changed the character of the war. It was no longer only a religious dispute but had become a political war. The French army and the Swedish army, both under excellent generals, won battle after battle. Soon the people of the war-torn German states began to cry for peace. For after thirty years of war the death and destruction were tremendous. More than one-third of the people in all the German states had died—over seven and a half million people. Hundreds of towns and villages had been destroyed. For the survivors the long years of poor harvests—or no harvests at all—had brought the food supply so low that starvation became a problem in many parts of Germany. Finally, after four years of discussion, the Thirty Years' War was brought to an end. The Treaty of Westphalia stated that Calvinism, Lutheranism, and Catholicism would thenceforth be acceptable religions in the German states. The prince of each German state was to be allowed to determine the religion of his own area. Each prince also was given the right to make agreements with other nations, for the German states were independent. Two new countries were recognized—the United Provinces (Holland)

and Switzerland became independent of the Hapsburgs. Although Richelieu had died before the peace was signed he would have been happy to know that his plan for France had been successful. France was granted, as her share in the victory, the two rich sections between present-day Germany and France—Alsace and Lorraine.

The next French king to rule after Louis XIII and Richelieu was Louis XIV. The English had at last succeeded in gaining the power to rule themselves through their parliament. But in France Louis XIV was determined to rule absolutely. He said, "I am the state," and he would let no one else have a say in the government. France was an absolute monarchy. Louis XIV ruled for seventy-two years. Not once during this long reign did France's parliament, called the Estates-General, meet. Whenever Louis needed money he collected it from his people—and he needed money often.

above left: Portrait of Louis XIV of France

Louis XIV was called the "Grand Monarch" or the "Sun King," for everything he did was to glorify himself. The people of France often thought of him as the leading character in a play rather than an ordinary human being. He wore corsets and a huge powdered wig and shoes with very high red heels that made him appear taller than he was. In spite of his fancy clothing, Louis made France the strongest nation in Europe. He was almost constantly fighting other countries, trying to increase the size of France and add to his kingdom. He fought several big wars and gained some land but always was stopped from going farther by alliances against him. England fought against him several times during his reign.

Louis built a magnificent palace not far from Paris—at a place called Versailles—in which there were marble halls, beautiful paintings, and many huge mirrors.

Louis not only surrounded himself with beautiful things, but also surrounded himself with the most interesting and creative men and women of his time. All those who could do anything exceptionally well—those who could paint well, write well, play well, or speak well—he brought together to live with him or near him. This was called his *court*. Those in his court were "in society."

This was fine for the people who were lucky enough to be in Louis' court. But the poor people of France—about ninety-five percent of the population—were the ones who had to pay Louis' expenses and those of his court. They had to pay for his parties and balls and feasts and for all the wars he fought. The last war had been fought on both land and sea—and the French had been defeated. France lost many of her colonies in America to England. Other countries gained land too.

Peter the Great of Russia

Russia is the largest country in the world, stretching from eastern Europe across Asia to China and Mongolia, and from the Arctic Circle to the Black Sea. Very little was known of Russia before the year 1700, for although it was a very large country, its people were divided into many different groups. The Russians are a branch of the Aryan race called Slavs, but they intermarried with the Mongol invaders and became like them in many ways. So that although the Russians were Christians, they were in every other way more Asiatic than European. The men wore long beards and long coats. The women wore veils like those the Turkish women wore. The people counted with balls strung on wires as the Chinese did. They even had a different alphabet. Russia was almost a separate world.

Then in 1694 a remarkable Russian prince came to the throne. His name was Peter. He completely changed Russia's thinking and way of life. Peter was very smart and very determined to make his country important in Europe. He began to make contacts with the West. In 1697 he went with a group of Russians to visit the West. In disguise, Peter visited England, Holland, Italy, and Austria. He studied art, schools, factories, and armies—everything done in the West that could be used to improve Russia. He returned to Russia with this knowledge. He also brought with him Europeans he had hired.

Peter then began to make Russia over. First of all, Peter wanted Russia to have a fleet of ships as other nations had. But in order to have a fleet he had to have a seaport for his ships, and Russia was landlocked; that is, she had no land bordering on water. Peter planned to take the land he needed from the neighboring country of Sweden.

The king of Sweden at this time was Charles XII. Charles was only eighteen years old, and Peter thought it would be an easy matter to win a war against this boy and help himself to whatever land he wanted. But Charles was an extraordinary boy. He was very bright and gifted, and had been unusually well educated. He knew several languages, he had learned to ride a horse when he was four years old, and he knew how to hunt and how to fight. Besides all this, he feared neither hardship nor danger—indeed, he was such a daredevil in battle that he was called the "Madman of the North," so at first Peter's army was beaten by Charles.

But Peter took his beating calmly, simply remarking that Charles would soon teach the Russian army how to win. Indeed, so successful was Charles at first in fighting Russia, Denmark, Prussia, and others who threatened him that the countries of Europe began to think of him as another Alexander the Great. They feared he might conquer them all. Charles became bolder and invaded Russia in 1709. But Peter had learned how to fight. The Swedish army was almost wiped out in a battle in the Ukraine at a place called Poltava (pool-tah'vuh). The war continued, but soon after Charles was killed in battle in Norway, Sweden gave up and a peace treaty was signed in 1721. This peace cost Sweden many provinces she had held in northern Germany, and also some land along the shore of the Baltic Sea.

Peter now had his seaport, his "window on the Baltic." He began to build ships and trade by land and sea with both the West and the Orient. He also built a great new city.

At this time the capital of Russia was Moscow. It was a beautiful city near the center of Russia, but far from the water and not very modern. This didn't suit Peter at all. For his capital he wanted a new city like the capitals he had visited in the West. He wanted it built on the water's edge, so that he could be close to this "window" to the West. Peter chose a spot near the Gulf of Finland, which was not only *on* the water but *under* water, for it was a marsh. A third of a million people, mostly serfs (peasants), were put to work filling in the marsh. On this new land Peter built a beautiful city with luxurious palaces, wide streets, and a fine harbor, plus many grand public buildings. This city he called St. Petersburg in honor of his patron saint, the apostle Peter, after whom he himself had been named. The name St. Petersburg was later changed to Petrograd and still later to Leningrad. (In 1917 the Russian capital was

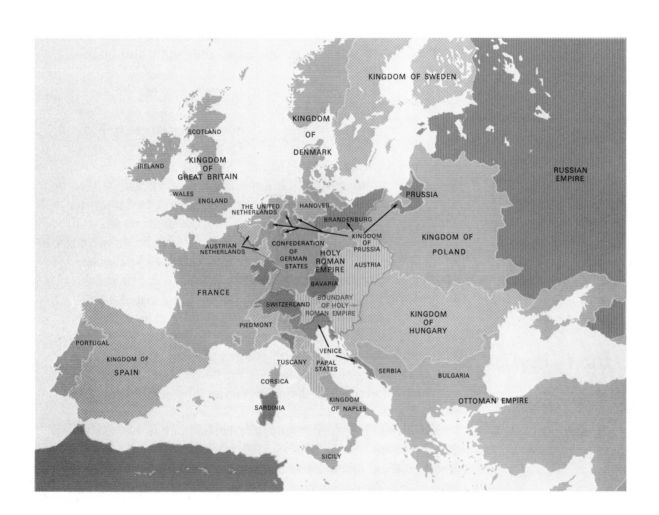

above: Europe in 1721

moved back to Moscow.) Peter passed new laws, started schools, and built factories and hospitals.

Peter westernized his country in another way too. He, like the kings of France, was an absolute monarch. All who opposed his rule were killed. He killed even his own son Alexis because he didn't agree with Peter's reforms. The serfs were little more than slaves. They were forced to work very hard and had practically no rights. Because he began to modernize Russia and make it a great power, this czar is called Peter the Great, the father of his country.

Frederick the Great of Prussia

Just as the Romanov family ruled in Russia, the Hohenzollern family ruled in Prussia. For generations the Hohenzollerns had increased their lands and power through war and marriage. During and after the Reformation they controlled widely scattered parts of Germany. Frederick William, called the Great Elector, was the first member of the family to exercise direct control of these holdings. He began to rule these scattered areas as one state, setting up an organization that enabled him to collect taxes, improve transportation, encourage business, and begin building an army.

In 1713 Frederick William I, grandson of the Great Elector, became king. Frederick William I was very mean and so tough that he was nicknamed the Sergeant King. He built up a very strong army. One regiment of this army was very unusual. The Potsdam Guards, as it was called, was made up of giants. This regiment was the king's passion, his hobby. Whenever he heard of a very tall man, no matter where the man might be and no matter what it might cost to get him, the Sergeant King bought, hired, or even kidnapped him for the Potsdam Guards. This collection of giants Frederick William made into a remarkable unit of soldiers—a unit of which he was very proud.

His son, Frederick, had curls and liked music, especially the flute, and dressed in fancy clothes. Frederick William was tough, but his son didn't seem capable of being a strong ruler. This disgusted his father, for he wanted his son to be as much interested in being a soldier and a fighter as he himself was.

Frederick, however, eventually turned out to be just the kind of man his father wanted him to be. He became a great soldier, fighter, and king, though he still loved poetry and music. Frederick wanted above everything else to make his country important in Europe.

One neighboring country of Prussia was Austria. In 1740 Austria was ruled by a woman named Maria Theresa. She had become ruler of Austria at the same time Frederick had become king of Prussia. At this time Maria Theresa held power over vast territories—Austria, Hungary, central Europe, northern Italy, and the Netherlands—and she had

opposite top: Frederick the Great, king of Prussia

opposite bottom: Queen Maria Theresa of Austria

support from the pope. In addition, Frederick's father had promised to leave Maria Theresa alone.

When Frederick became king, however, he wanted to add a part of Austria to his own country, and he simply helped himself to the piece of Maria Theresa's country that he wanted. Of course this started a war. Before long almost every country in Europe was fighting—either with Frederick or against him. But Frederick succeeded not only in getting what he was after, but also succeeded in holding on to it.

Maria Theresa, however, would not give up. She wanted to get back what had been taken away from her. So quietly and secretly she began to get ready for another war against Frederick. She persuaded other countries to promise to help her, but before she was ready Frederick heard what she was doing and suddenly attacked her again. This war lasted seven years, from 1756 to 1763, and naturally was called the Seven Years' War. Frederick kept on fighting until he had beaten Austria for good. Thus he gained his purpose, which was to make his country important and powerful.

Frederick still held on to the part of Austria that he had at first taken away from Maria Theresa. Maria Theresa was a great queen, and she would have won against Frederick had he been an ordinary king. But Frederick was one of the world's smartest generals and was too much for her. Because he did so much for Prussia he is called Frederick the Great.

The Seven Years' War, strange to say, was fought not only in Europe but also in far-off America. England had taken Frederick's side. France and her allies were against him. So the English settlers in America, who were on Frederick's side, fought the French settlers, who were against him. In America this was called the French and Indian War. When Frederick won in Europe, the English in America won against the French in America. Because of this war Americans speak English today instead of French. If Frederick had lost and France had won, Americans probably would speak French instead of English. As one of the conditions of the peace treaty signed in 1763 France gave up to England, Frederick's ally, Canada and land west of the Mississippi River.

Heroic soldier gallops off alone to survey enemy territory at the Battle of Rossbach during the Seven Years' War

The American Revolution

By the early eighteenth century, most European states were ruled by monarchs. Except for England, these rulers were unchecked. They ruled absolutely and made laws as they saw fit. This could be good or bad for the common people.

Late in the 1700's, Europe had several monarchs who were called "enlightened despots." Because they did many things to improve the conditions of their subjects they were called enlightened; because they ruled absolutely they were called despots. Among the most notable of these rulers were Catherine the Great of Russia, Joseph II of Austria, and Frederick the Great of Prussia. Each to some degree tried to improve education, roads, laws, and the economic and religious conditions in their nations. Each was successful in a very small way. Time would show, however, that this little bit of success would not be enough to stop the new political attitudes that were becoming more and more popular.

Much of this new thinking came from the writings of men like John Locke, Charles Montesquieu, and Adam Smith. Each promoted the right of man to determine how he should be ruled in both his political life and his business life. These ideas were accepted eagerly by the middle class—businessmen, tradesmen, and professional people—and rejected by the monarchs because they were a danger to their absolute rule. These ideas would first be put into practice not in the old world, but in the new. And again the English people were to be champions of liberty.

The first truly born and bred Englishman to become king was George III. When he came to the throne in 1760 he wanted to cooperate closely with Parliament in the rule of his lands.

As George looked over his holdings, he saw that for a long time the American colonies had been fairly independent. So he began to tighten his control over them. Together with Parliament, George began to enforce more strictly all British laws and regulations. He added new taxes and collected money for the cost of running the government both at home and abroad.

Since the founding of the first two little settlements, or colonies, the English holdings had grown in number, size, and wealth, until in 1763 they stretched along the coast of the Atlantic. The majority of people settled there were English. They were freedom-loving people, but they were loyal subjects of the king. Several things made the American colonists different from their forefathers, however. First, because of the 3000-mile distance between them and their king, it was very difficult for England to control them. Also, in America there were opportunities for the colonists to improve themselves despite what may have been their humble beginnings; these opportunities did not exist in England.

For ten years the American colonists resisted the efforts of their king to tax them or otherwise limit their freedom. They objected to the fact that such laws, especially tax laws, were passed without their consent or approval.

Through speeches, such leaders as Patrick Henry and Samuel Adams aroused support for the defense of colonial rights. They also demonstrated publicly and sometimes violently.

One such demonstration took place in 1773 when Boston had a "tea party." Dressed as Indians, the colonists boarded three British ships in Boston Harbor in the dark of night. They hurled the cargo of tea into the water. This was their way of showing the king and his agents that they would not pay a tax on tea.

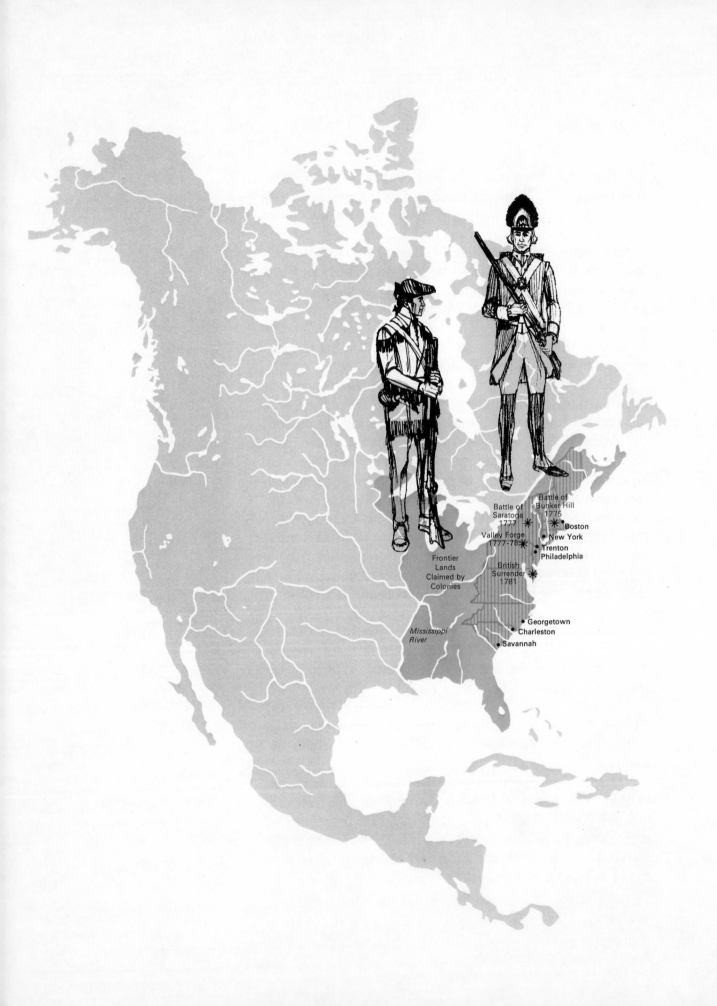

Battle of
Saratoga
1777

Battle of
Bunker Hill
1775

Boston

Valley Forge
1777-78

New York

Trenton

Philadelphia

Frontier
Lands
Claimed by
Colonies

British
Surrender
1781

Mississippi
River

Georgetown

Charleston

Savannah

The colonists continued to hold meetings and discussions in attempts to get the king and the English Government to listen to their demands. Representatives of each colony appeared unofficially at many of these meetings.

Even one of America's greatest public servants was unable to convince the king. This talented and extraordinary man was Benjamin Franklin. A printer, writer, inventor, and scientist, Franklin had long been active in colonial affairs. When the disputes began he was sent to England. He spoke to the English Parliament, putting forth the colonists' objections to taxation without representation. But he failed. Finally Franklin knew it was useless for him to remain in England. He returned home just in time for the beginning of the armed resistance that began America's revolution.

Franklin, as we have said, was very active in the new government. So was a man named Thomas Jefferson. He wrote a paper called the Declaration of Independence. It declared that citizens want a government to protect them. It listed the ways England had failed to do this for America and stated that, therefore, the colonies had the right to become independent of England. Fifty-six Americans, including Benjamin Franklin, were chosen by the people to sign the Declaration of Independence. He is the only man to have signed not only this document, but also every other important document of the time. Realizing that signing the Declaration of Independence was an open act of treason, Franklin is reported to have advised his fellow signers and countrymen that "We must indeed all hang together or assuredly we shall hang separately." The men signed it anyway. The signing of this paper, however, did not make England give up the colonies. King George's armies still tried to stop the colonies from leaving England's rule.

The people in America, finding that talking did no good, started to fight. This fight was called the American Revolution. The leader of the revolution was a man named George Washington. He was honest and brave, had a good mind, loved his country, and was a good fighter.

Washington had a very small army with which to fight the English army, and very little money with which to pay the soldiers. He had a hard time supplying them with food, clothing, powder, or shot. During the winter of 1776-1777 the soldiers nearly froze and starved to death in Valley Forge, for they had too little of everything soldiers need to

A painting of George Washington by Gilbert Stuart

Map shows some of the major battles of the American Revolution fight a war. It seemed as if the war could not go on unless they received help. Yet Washington kept up their spirits.

Benjamin Franklin was once again sent across the ocean —this time to try to get the necessary help. He went to France, for France hated England because she had lost Canada and part of America to England at the end of the Seven Years' War. But at first France would not help. She took little interest in the fight, for Washington's army had lost a number of battles against the English. In 1778, however—the year after the Declaration of Independence was signed—the American army beat the English at a place called Saratoga in New York State. Then the king of France became more interested and sent help to the colonies so they could carry on the war. A young French nobleman named Lafayette went to help the Americans and fought under General Washington. He made a great name for himself.

England, seeing that things were going against her, now wanted to make peace with the Americans and give them the same rights as English citizens. But it was too late. The Americans would agree to nothing less than complete independence from England, so the war continued.

As we have said, the English had been beaten by the Yankees, as they called the American soldiers, in the North at Saratoga. So an English general, Lord Cornwallis, was sent to the South to try to win there. A man named General Greene was put in command of the southern American soldiers. Lord Cornwallis tried to fight Greene, but Greene led him a merry chase around the country. In 1781, in a little place called Yorktown in Virginia, Cornwallis and his army finally were surrounded and could not escape. On the land was the American army, and on the water were the French warships that had been sent over to help in the war. Cornwallis had to surrender.

King George then said, "Let us have peace." In 1783, eight years after it had started, the war ended when a treaty of peace was signed. The colonies now were independent of England. They organized a republic and called themselves the United States of America. The thirteen stripes on the American flag are reminders of the courage and bravery of the thirteen original colonies.

The first American government didn't work out well because it didn't have enough authority to enforce the laws or to make the states work well together. A new constitution was written and accepted by the states in 1789. This new

above: The French nobleman Lafayette who fought under General George Washington during the American Revolution

constitution formed a government that had three parts, or branches. The *legislative* branch, or lawmaking body, was a Congress made up of representatives of the states. The *judicial* branch was made up of the courts that would judge the laws and protect the rights of the citizens. The *executive* branch was headed by the president—a man elected to lead the government.

George Washington was the first President of the United States; for this reason he is called "the father of his country—first in war, first in peace, and first in the hearts of his countrymen."

For the next one hundred years, America followed the advice of George Washington and stayed out of European affairs. Her interests were devoted to building up her industry, expanding settlements to the west, and defeating enemies that hoped to stop her progress.

below: American and English soldiers at battle during the American Revolution

The French Revolution

The people in France saw how successful the Americans had been in their fight against the king of England, and not long after the American Revolution they rebelled against their own king and the absolute monarchy in France.

The reason the French people rebelled against their king was that they had very little, and the king and his royal family and nobles seemed to have everything. Both the Americans and the French rebelled against being taxed without their consent. The Americans rebelled because of principle as much as anything else. Their taxes had not been very high, but they thought them unjust. The French taxes, however, not only were unjust but they took almost everything the people had. They had to pay a tax on their land and their income. There were also taxes for the up-keep of the church, and even taxes to the lords that went back to feudal times. Also, under this government, there was very little freedom of religion, speech, or writing—and it was almost impossible for a man to earn a better life or a better job. The government interfered with trade and industry.

We have seen how bad things were under Louis XIV. They became worse and worse until the people could stand it no longer. Wars, waste, and corrupt kings after Louis XIV continued to make life hard for the common people. Perhaps Louis XV, the last king before the revolution, knew how bad things were. Before he died, he is reported to have said, "After me, the deluge." How right he was.

In 1774 the king of France was Louis XVI, and his queen was Marie Antoinette. Although the people were so poor they had hardly anything to eat except very coarse and bad-tasting black bread, they were compelled to pay heavy taxes to support the king and the nobles so that they could live in fine style. They were forced to work for them for little or no pay. If anyone complained, he could be put in prison until he died.

Neither the king nor his wife were really wicked. They were young and thoughtless. They meant well, but like a great many well-meaning people, they lacked common sense and did not know how others lived. They didn't seem to understand that people could be poor, for they had so much themselves.

The country was in bad shape because Louis XIV and XV had conducted long wars and had lived very extravagantly. Louis XVI was forced to call for more money. He tried many ways but the court of Paris said that no taxes could be collected unless representatives of the people agreed. So for the first time in over one hundred and seventy-five years, the Estates-General was called. They met in May, 1789.

This group was divided into three classes, or Estates, found in France. The First Estate was the clergy, the Second the nobility, and the Third and largest (about ninety percent of the population) was the middle class—the commoners and peasants. The clergy and the nobility had many privileges and few duties or taxes. The Third Estate was overworked and overtaxed. They wanted real reform.

When the Estates-General met, it was customary for each Estate, or group, to meet separately and discuss the issues and problems. After talking, each group would decide how they wanted to vote. Then they would vote as a group. Under this system, each Estate was allowed to cast only one vote—so there were three votes in all.

The First and Second Estates usually voted the same way because they wanted to protect their privileges. The Third Estate, knowing that they would be outvoted, insisted that everyone meet together and vote as individuals. Refusing to meet under any other conditions, the Third Estate forced the king to do things their way. They now would have the help of the members of the other two classes who were sympathetic toward them.

Louis XVI of France

This new government body was called the National Assembly. They tried to work out some plan to do away with the injustices the people had been suffering. They wanted everyone to be free and equal with a voice in the government.

The people of Paris became furious and revolted in anger when they learned that Louis was gathering an army that might be used to stop the Assembly. A wild and angry mob attacked the old prison called the Bastille, which was to them a symbol of all the injustices they had suffered. Under the battle cry "Storm the Bastille!" they battered down the gates, freed the prisoners, and killed the guards because they were servants of the king.

The Bastille was stormed on July 14, 1789. This was the beginning of what is called the French Revolution. Today Bastille Day is a holiday in France.

Lafayette, the French hero of the American Revolution, was now back in France. He led the people's army that was formed in Paris. This force was called the National Guard. Riots spread to the country where homes of nobles were burned. Also, most records and deeds were destroyed.

Queen Marie Antoinette, wife of Louis XVI of France

Meanwhile, the National Assembly drew up what was called a Declaration of the Rights of Man, which was something like the American Declaration of Independence. It said that all men were born free and equal and it guaranteed freedom of speech, press, and religion. It said the people should make the laws. It also abolished many of the privileges the upper classes had had previously. The laws should be the same for all, the taxes would be shared by all, and all men had the right to a fair trial.

Soon after the Declaration of Rights had been made, the mob from Paris marched the ten miles to Versailles, where Louis and Marie Antoinette lived and where the Assembly were meeting. Ragged and wild-looking, they carried sticks and stones and cried, "Bread, bread!" as they marched. Up the beautiful grand staircase of the palace they rushed. The few guards remaining with the king were unable to hold them back. The mob captured the king and queen and took them back to Paris.

By 1791 the National Assembly had drawn up a constitution—a set of rules by which the country would be governed justly. This the king agreed to and signed. The constitution limited the king's power. Laws would be made by the Assembly. The king would keep his title but would lose his power to make laws. He would have to go along with the wishes of the people. Louis didn't really like this constitution, the nobles didn't like it, and the countries outside of France didn't like it. Remember they were absolute monarchies, and ideas such as those of the French Revolution were dangerous to them. Still things might have worked out if the king had not tried to leave France with his wife and family. He was captured and brought back to Paris in chains. The people decided to do away with the king entirely, both in name and in fact. The monarchy was abolished and a republic was established. The king and queen were put in prison. They stayed there until 1793, when Louis was tried for treason, found guilty, and sentenced to death.

above left: Robespierre, leader of the Reign of Terror in France

opposite: Robespierre and his fellow conspirators are sent to the guillotine

At this time, a new machine had been invented by a Frenchman named Guillotine. He named the machine after himself. It had a heavy blade that would slide down and chop off a person's head. It was more efficient and quicker than an ax. The guillotine had a great deal of use after the French Revolution, for the mob was not satisfied even after Louis' death. They feared all those who were in favor of kings and executed many, many people. Even the poor inventor, Mr. Guillotine, was killed with his own machine. He was executed for the crime of inventing such a horrible machine!

Now began what is called the Reign of Terror. A man named Robespierre (roh-behs-pyair') and two of his friends were leaders in this Reign of Terror. They began to arrest and behead anyone suspected of being in favor of kings. The queen was one of the first to be beheaded. Many nobles and priests were killed. Anyone who disagreed with the new government was killed. Things got so bad that if one even whispered, "there's a man, or there's a woman, or there's a child who is in favor of kings," that person would be sent to the guillotine. No one was sure of his life for a day. One never knew when he might be accused by some personal enemy. Hundreds, then thousands, of suspected people were beheaded.

People seemed to have gone wild, crazy, mad! They insulted God and the Christian religion. They put a pretty woman called the Goddess of Reason on the altar of the beautiful Church of Notre Dame and worshipped her. They pulled down statues and pictures of Jesus and the Virgin Mary. In their places they put statues and pictures of their own leaders. The guillotine was put up in place of the cross. They did away with Sundays. They made the week ten days long, and made every tenth day a holiday instead of Sunday. They stopped counting time from Jesus' birth, because they didn't want anything to do with Christianity; they began to call the year 1792, when the republic was started, the year 1. But none of these things lasted very long.

At last the people, in fear of Robespierre, a monstrous and inhuman tyrant, rose up against him. In July, 1794, Robespierre went to the same death to which he had sent countless others and the Reign of Terror was ended. Though it had lasted only ten months, thousands had died.

left: The oldest existing globe

below: A model of the **Santa María,** the ship used by Christopher Columbus in 1492

opposite: A portrait of Christopher Columbus

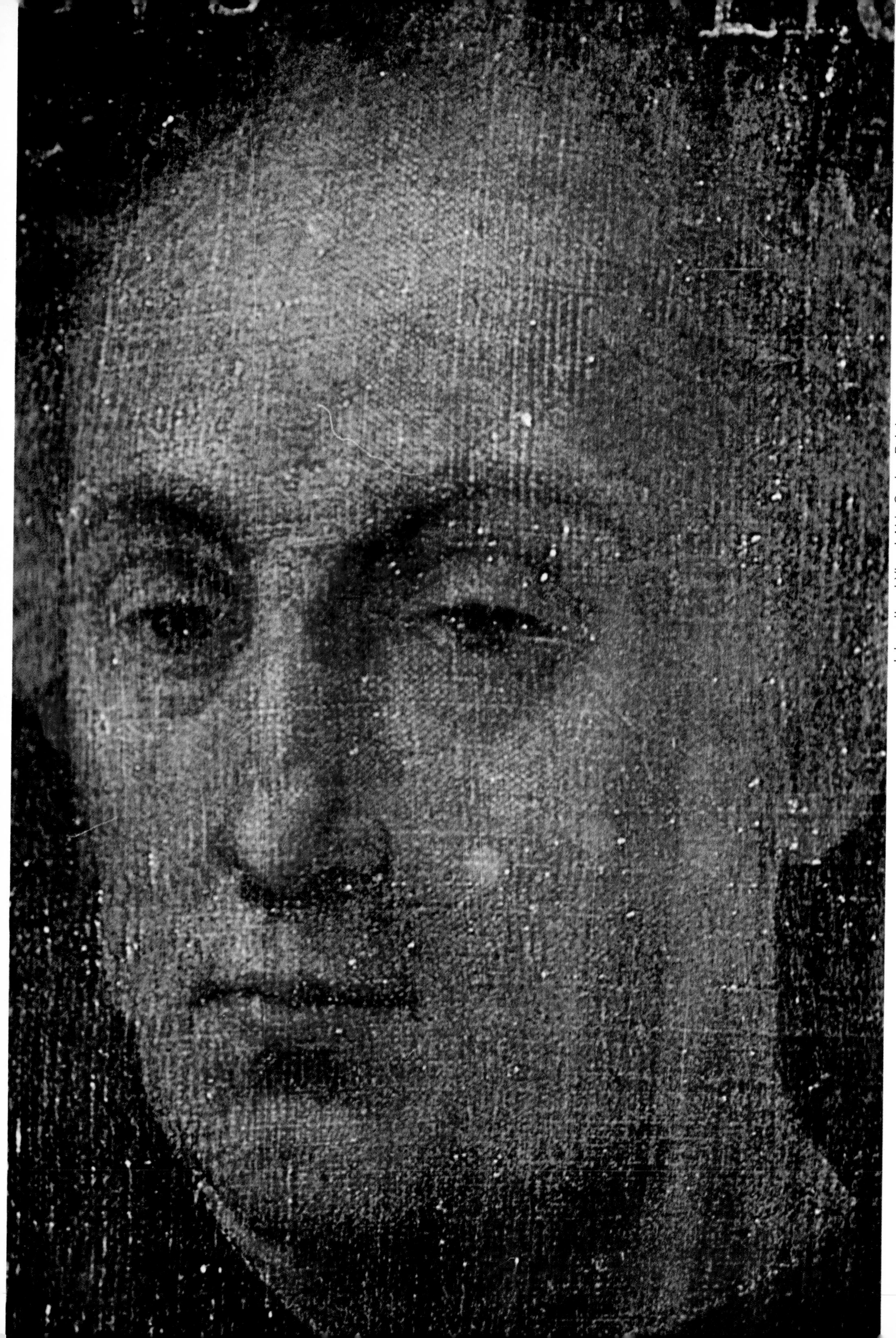

International Visual Aids Center, Belgium

opposite: A portrait of Henry VIII, king of England, painted by Holbein

left: The explorer Ferdinand Magellan discovers the strait at the tip of South America

above: The armor worn by Charles V of France when he was a child

69

above and opposite: Charles V, King of France, makes a solemn entry into Bruges, Belgium

above: A fifteenth-century French sculpture

opposite: The development of firearms

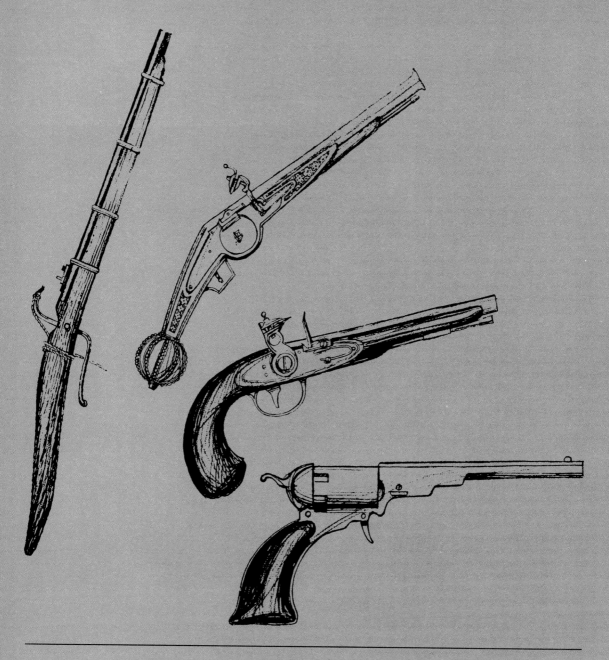

clockwise from above:

The first hand-held gun—an early fifteenth-century matchlock. In order for the gun to fire, a cord had to be put through a hole at the rear of the barrel and then lit. The cord burned slowly down to the gunpowder, which then exploded.

A late fifteenth- or early sixteenth-century wheel-lock gun. The ball on the end could be used as a club or mace in hand-to-hand combat.

An eighteenth-century flintlock pistol

A nineteenth-century American repeating pistol that used rimfire percussion cartridges

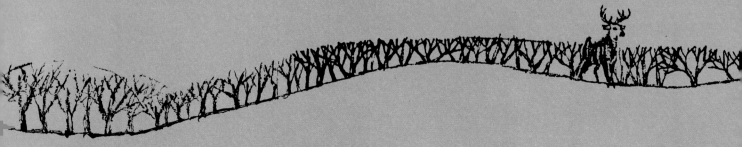

opposite: A model of
the **Mayflower,** the ship
that brought the
Pilgrims to the New
World

left: The Green Mountain
Boys—frontiersmen from
Vermont who fought in
the American Revolution

right: Early techniques for sighting or aiming cannon depended on a combination of crude geometry and skillful guesswork. The Spanish cannoneers shown here are using gunner's levels in their efforts to aim accurately at pirateers on the Caribbean.

opposite: A model of an English 50-gun ship

Bob Brunton—Hollis Associates

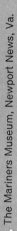

left: The Spirit of St. Louis, the airplane in which Charles Lindbergh made the first solo flight across the Atlantic Ocean in 1927

above: Astronaut Edward H. White during his spectacular walk in space on June 3, 1965

above: During the American Revolution, the Irish Volunteers protected Ireland from invaders

above: Early nineteenth-century Turkish tapestry

Napoleon: The Little Giant

In 1795 the new government, the Directory, was holding a meeting in Paris when a mob in the streets outside began rioting. A young captain was given a few men and told to keep the mob away. The young officer pointed cannons down each street that led to the palace, and no one dared to show himself. The man was named Napoleon Bonaparte. He made such a fine show in this first command that he was sent to command the French army in Italy. This man, who was only five feet tall, became a general at twenty-six. In four years he was to become sole ruler of France.

Napoleon had been born in 1769 on the little island of Corsica in the Mediterranean Sea.

At this time all the other countries of Europe had kings —absolute monarchs like Louis had been. France had caught the fever of revolution from America and had removed her king. The kings of the other countries were afraid their people might revolt too, so all these other countries became enemies of France because France had put an end to her monarchy.

Napoleon was sent off to fight Italy. He crossed the Alps just as Hannibal had done during the Punic Wars long before. But Hannibal had no heavy cannons and it seemed impossible for Napoleon's army to cross these treacherous mountains with cannons. Napoleon asked his engineers, the men who were supposed to know about such things, if it could be done. They said they thought it was impossible.

"Impossible," Napoleon angrily replied, "is a word found only in the dictionary of fools." Then he shouted: "There shall be no Alps!" and went ahead and crossed them. His army won in Italy, and he signed a peace with Austria in 1797 in which northern Italy was given to France. Returning to France, Napoleon was greeted by the people as a conquering hero.

The men who were then governing France—the Directory—were afraid of him. They feared he might try to make himself king because he was so popular with the people. Napoleon asked to be sent to conquer Egypt. He was sure he could get the better of the English there, and if he did he planned to cut England off from India, the new country they had invaded in the reign of James I.

The French government was glad of the chance to get rid of Napoleon, so they sent him off to Egypt. Napoleon quickly conquered Egypt, as Julius Caesar had done, but at the same time he suffered serious defeats. While he was conquering Egypt, his fleet, which was waiting for him at the mouth of the Nile, was caught and destroyed by an English fleet under one of the greatest admirals of all time —Lord Nelson.

Napoleon had no way to take his army back to France, so he left another general in command and managed to find a ship to take him back home. When he reached France he kept very quiet about this naval defeat. He was again a hero.

Upon his return, Napoleon found that the men who were supposed to be governing were quarreling among themselves. Seeing his chance, he seized power. He forced three directors to retire and with the help of the army arrested the remaining two. Taking power by military force is called a *coup d'etat* (kood-eh-tah'), which means a stroke of state.

Only ten years after the Revolution, in 1799, Napoleon formed a new government with a new constitution. The people of France agreed to this government. They were tired of conflict and wanted safety and peace, so they let Napoleon become a dictator. Five years later he became emperor of France. He was one of three men chosen to rule France. He was called First Consul. There were two assistant consuls, but the assistants were little more than clerks to do Napoleon's bidding. It was only a very short time before Napoleon was made First Consul for life.

The other countries of Europe began to fear that Napoleon would conquer them, too, and make them a part of France, so they joined together to try to defeat him. Napoleon planned to conquer England first, and he prepared to send a fleet across the English Channel. He knew that as long as England controlled the sea, France would never be safe from invasion. In 1805 his fleet was caught off Spain near a point called Trafalgar by Lord Nelson, the same English admiral who had beaten him in Egypt. Napoleon's fleet was utterly destroyed, though Nelson himself was killed.

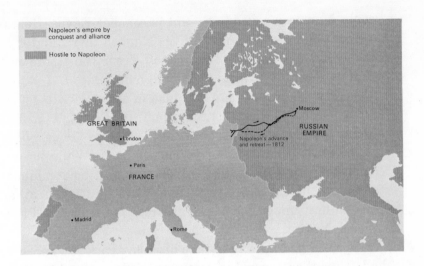

GREAT BRITAIN

•London

•Moscow

RUSSIAN EMPIRE

Napoleon's advance and retreat—1812

•Paris

FRANCE

•Madrid

•Rome

above right: The empire of Napoleon

opposite: **Napoleon in his study,** a painting by Jacques Louis David

Napoleon then gave up the idea of conquering England and turned his attention in the opposite direction. One at a time he beat the countries in Europe who were allied against him. Austria, Prussia, and Russia were forced to agree to his terms of peace.

In 1810 Napoleon was at the height of his power in Europe. He ruled Spain and Denmark and controlled Sweden and Italy and the little states of Germany. Almost all of Europe either belonged to him or accepted French leadership. But the empire was too big. First there was trouble in Austria; then in 1812 Spain, with English help, broke free. At the same time, on the other side of the French Empire, Russia—under Alexander—broke the French naval blockade of the Baltic Sea. In order to keep his allies in line, Napoleon had to keep England out of the Baltic, so he declared war on Russia. This proved to be a fatal mistake.

The Russians didn't meet the French army in the open. They kept pulling back, drawing Napoleon's army deeper into Russia, burning everything that might be helpful to the invaders—even Moscow itself. Even though Moscow was captured, it was no victory—the Russian army was still undefeated. Then the horrible, long Russian winter began. Without food or shelter Napoleon was forced to retreat. It was terribly cold; there were deep snows and his retreating army suffered enormous losses. Napoleon left his army to get back the best way they could and returned to Paris. The stranded men and animals died of cold and hunger by the thousands, and thousands more were killed by Russian guerrillas. Napoleon reached Paris, but his fortune had turned. All of Europe, under England's leader-

ship, was arming to put an end to the tyrant. Napoleon was defeated at Leipzig in 1813. This battle is called the "Battle of Nations."

In 1814 Napoleon was forced to promise to give up his throne, leave France, and go to live on the little island of Elba, just off the coast of Italy. Napoleon, however, was not yet finished. He was determined to return to France and regain his throne.

Napoleon managed to leave Elba without being caught and landed on the coast of France in 1815. The French government at Paris sent an army of Napoleon's old soldiers against him with orders to meet him and bring him to Paris in an iron cage. But when the soldiers met their old general they went over to his side, and with them he marched on Paris. For a hundred days Napoleon again ruled as emperor. But European armies north of France were preparing to fight. Napoleon quickly got together an army and went forth to meet them. At a little town called Waterloo, in Belgium, Napoleon fought his last battle. He was beaten completely there by an English general named Wellington and a Prussian general named Blucher. It was the year 1815 and Napoleon was finished for good; he had met his great defeat at Waterloo. Today, when someone is defeated or has an insurmountable problem we say he has "met his Waterloo."

After Waterloo, the English took Napoleon away and put him on a little island in the middle of the South Atlantic Ocean—an island from which he could not possibly escape. This lonely spot was named St. Helena after the mother of Constantine. Here Napoleon lived for six years before he died in 1821.

Many of Napoleon's accomplishments were lasting, however; his civil law, or Code of Napoleon, is still the basis of French law today.

The French Revolution and Napoleon caused a tremendous change in Europe in only twenty-five years. The ideas of liberty, equality, and fraternity were held by many.

People believed in their right to choose their government. They also held that governments of nations should consider all the people and provide for education, security, justice, religious freedom, and economic opportunities.

These ideas were spread by Napoleon's conquering army to Germany, Italy, and Spain. The laws Napoleon had passed furthered these ideas.

Europe Moves toward National Unity

Napoleon was gone. In 1814 the leaders of the nations that had defeated him met in the city of Vienna to sign a peace treaty with France and also to remake the map of Europe, for Napoleon had conquered almost the entire continent. He had set up his own governments under his own hand-picked people. Now new governments had to take over. The Congress of Vienna determined how this was to be done.

Although there were many men at this meeting, the most important man was an Austrian prince named Metternich. This man hated all the democratic ideas that the French Revolution stood for. He wanted to turn the clock back and have countries run by monarchs. He convinced the kings of Europe that this was the only way they could avoid having revolutions in their own countries. Completely ignoring what the people wanted, which was self-government and union with their own national group, England, Russia, Prussia, and Austria went to work.

Within a short time, the European powers—led by Metternich—were engaged in putting down dozens of small uprisings across the continent. The nations were successful in quelling revolutions in Italy, Spain, France, some German states, and Poland. To prevent further trouble, no freedom of speech, press, or education was allowed. Spys were used everywhere to report on all possible revolts. Still revolts continued. People could not forget that they had once had rights.

Only a few of the many revolts were successful. In 1829 the Greeks succeeded in throwing out the Turks and setting up their own government. About the same time the colonies in the Americas that had once belonged to Spain also were freed. This was made possible because of help given by the United States. When it looked as if the European powers were going to send troops across the Atlantic, the American president issued a warning to the European monarchs. This document was called the Monroe Doctrine, and said in effect: "You stay out of our affairs and we will stay out of yours. If you interfere in the western hemisphere, it will come to war." Realizing they had no chance of regaining possessions, the European nations honored the Monroe Doctrine.

Finally the French people decided they had had enough of kings. In 1848, in disgust, they threw out their last king—Louis Philippe. A new government was set up by a French assembly. It was the second republic to be headed by a president chosen by the people.

The French people elected Napoleon's nephew as their president. He had planned and plotted again and again to make himself king of France, but again and again he had failed. And now he was elected president! But Louis Napoleon didn't want to be just a president. He wanted to be like his uncle, the great Napoleon. He dreamed of being emperor and conquering Europe, and in 1851 he used his army to take over the state. The next year he made himself an absolute ruler and formed the Second Empire. He called himself Napoleon III.

For awhile Napoleon was popular with the people, but as time passed, he did many things they did not like. But it was Napoleon's errors in dealing with Prussia that would cause his overthrow.

Napoleon III was jealous of the neighboring country of German states that were about to be unified by France's rival power—Prussia.

At this time there were many states in Germany. These states decided to join together in a confederation. This confederation was like a club, but the states didn't really work together. In fact, the two biggest members didn't even like each other. Austria was elected president of the German Confederation, but Austria wasn't interested in uniting the states into a nation like France or England. This was because most of her people weren't even German. The Austrian Empire was made up of Poles, Hungarians, Slavic people, and Italians.

Prussia, on the other hand, was made up of only Germans. Prussia wanted all Germans to work together economically and politically. She didn't want Austria to have anything to do with German affairs.

While Napoleon III ruled in France, William I ruled in Prussia. William was helped by a leading German statesman named Bismarck. Bismarck had great plans for his nation. He intended to make it rich and powerful. To do this, he had to defeat his enemies both at home and also in other countries.

Otto von Bismarck was not interested in democratic ways. He knew that what he wanted would not be achieved by talking. He said that only "blood and iron" would make Prussia strong, and he began to build up an army.

He used this army against Austria in 1866. This war lasted only seven weeks, and in this short time Austria was completely defeated. From now on, Prussia would be the leader of the German states and a new club, called the North German Confederation, was formed.

This was only one step in Bismarck's plan. He wanted a unified Germany led by Prussia. But some large southern German States—Bavaria, Württemberg, Baden, and Hesse—were afraid of Prussia and they wouldn't join Bismarck.

As Bismarck thought about this problem he had a very sneaky idea. He knew that if he had a war with a foreign power, the southern states would come to his side. After all, they were proud and they wouldn't let an outsider get the better of them. Once they were united for war, it would be very easy to keep them united to form a union with Prussia. So Bismarck waited for his chance.

In 1870, his chance finally came. The people in Spain had thrown out their king. They wanted a new one and they were thinking of asking a Prussian prince to take the throne. This frightened Napoleon III of France, for he

above left: The German statesman, Otto von Bismarck

above: Napoleon III, emperor of France

top to bottom:

Italian revolutionist Garibaldi

Victor Emmanuel II, king of Sardinia, who was later to become king of Italy

Count Cavour, Prime Minister of Sardinia

didn't want to have Prussian rulers on both sides of him. To stop this from happening, he demanded that the Prussian king promise never to allow any of his family to accept the Spanish throne. This demand made the king very angry. Using the latest invention, the telegram, he sent a message to Bismarck.

This message, called the Ems dispatch, became very important because Bismarck took the king's message and rearranged the facts to make the French look foolish. Then he published it in the French papers. When the French people read the "dispatch" they were furious, and they rioted. Napoleon III was forced to declare war against Prussia on July 19, 1870.

Napoleon and the French armies were completely beaten by Prussia. The Prussians marched into Paris and Napoleon was sent to live in England. The Prussians demanded very hard peace terms. France had to give them some land that bordered the two countries. She also had to pay them more than a billion dollars, and until she paid, Prussian soldiers would stay in France. To the amazement of everybody, the French were able to pay this debt within three years.

The most important outcome of this war was that Prussia was able to bring together the German Confederation of States into a unified and very strong nation—called Germany for the first time. William became emperor and was called Kaiser. He was crowned in the magnificent French Palace at Versailles.

But this war was not really ended. The complete defeat and surrender of the French was humiliating to them and the hard peace terms were worse.

France formed a new republic with a president. She began to build up her army so that next time she would be ready for the Germans.

The activities of France, Austria, and Prussia influenced the course of events in Italy. For this country, like the old German states, was made up of many separate parts. Some parts were ruled by France and some by the pope. But after the era of Napoleon, Italy began to try to unite.

The first revolutions were not successful, but the ideas of unity and nationalism were to continue to grow. The king of Sardinia, Victor Emmanuel II, was an important leader in this series of revolutions. He was to continue to support the idea that Italy should be free from foreigners. This

The meeting of Garibaldi and Victor Emmanuel

king was aided by his Prime Minister, Count Cavour. Together they began to plan for the unification of Italy.

The most dramatic and outstanding revolutionist was a man named Garibaldi. Once a poor immigrant candle maker in New York, Garibaldi returned to his country to lead his people to freedom. He was a popular man and when he called for soldiers to fight, they flocked to his side. In 1860 Garibaldi was able to invade successfully both Sicily and Naples, in the southern part of the Italian peninsula. As he marched north, the people continued to join Garibaldi and the "red shirts" as his troops were called. Although Garibaldi favored a republic in the interests of his country, he agreed to give in to Victor Emmanuel. In 1861, Victor Emmanuel was crowned king of Italy.

Still one important section of the country was missing. Rome had for hundreds of years been the property of the pope and this city was protected by the French. But in 1870, when the French were being beaten by the Prussians, they were unable to help Rome. Victor Emmanuel took the city and made it the capital of a new united kingdom of Italy.

At last these three—Victor Emmanuel, Cavour, and Garibaldi—succeeded in making their country one big nation.

Austria had lost land in Italy when the Italian states had revolted and she had lost leadership of the German states to Prussia. Still she controlled a large empire in which there was a vast variety of peoples—Germans, Magyars (Hungarians), Czechs, Poles, Rumanians, and Slavs. These people continued to express their desire for recognition as national groups and national states. To meet these demands in part and to strengthen Austrian power, the empire was changed in 1867. The largest national group in the empire, the Magyars, was allowed to form its own government with its own lawmaking body, or parliament. This part of Austria became Hungary. Because both nations shared the same king, the new nation was called Austria-Hungary.

In Russia, the czars were still absolute monarchs but they were having difficulty controlling the country because the people were very unhappy. So, in 1861, Czar Alexander II freed the Russian serfs or farm workers. Yet this was not enough to satisfy the people and within the next fifty years the nation was to be shattered by revolution and disorder.

Moving east across the vast spaces of Russia, we come to the ancient land of China. This country, after centuries of isolation, was beginning to be drawn into conflicts with the Western powers. Her government was not strong and after a series of wars with Japan and England she was forced to allow foreigners to settle and trade along great areas of her coast.

Just off the Chinese mainland is a group of islands that make up Japan—the land of the rising sun. Japan had a government that had ruled for centuries. She also kept Westerners out of her country for many, many years. But in 1854, this situation was changed. In that year an American naval officer named Commodore Perry came to Japan. He persuaded the Japanese government to sign a treaty agreeing to protect shipwrecked American sailors. After this, other treaties were made and trade began between Japan and the Western world.

During the time of revolutions and national movements on the European continent, a famous queen—Victoria—was on the English throne. From 1837 to 1901, Victoria ruled an empire made up of a chain of colonies around the globe. Some of the now-independent states that made up this empire were Canada, Australia, New Zealand, New-

Other Nations Develop

foundland, South Africa, and India. So outstanding was this woman that the period of her rule is known as the Victorian Age.

English monarchs since 1688 had accepted rule by Parliament, so although Victoria was queen she didn't really make the decisions. The real governing was done by the prime minister. This position, according to English tradition, was given to the man who had the most votes in Parliament. He was chosen by his fellow members. So the monarch reigns in England, but the prime minister rules. During Victoria's reign, England had several notable prime ministers. Each advanced English power and also her democracy.

The people of England were influenced by the revolutions that were shaking the continent. They did not desire another type of government, however, or another monarch. They wanted only the right to vote. At the beginning of the eighteenth century only five percent of the population had the right to vote. But by the close of that century, the vote had been given to most of the male wage earners, and the government in England had become democratic.

Across the Atlantic Ocean, the United States of America continued to develop. This young nation during the late 1800's provided a new home for thousands and thousands of immigrants who had failed to achieve freedom at home and sought a place in this growing country.

As the nation developed to the west and new states were formed there arose conflict over the question of whether these new areas should enter the Union as slave states or free states. The South wanted the new states to accept slavery and the North wanted them to be free. There was violent disagreement over the question, until finally in 1861 the southern states declared their independence. They left the Union and formed a new government called the Confederate States of America. The northern states, led by President Abraham Lincoln, said that the Union of the United States could not be broken up. The southern states had no right to leave and would be breaking the law as stated in the Constitution to do so. A civil war began over the question.

This war lasted for four years. From 1861 to 1865 the nation was torn by constant fighting. In 1865 the North was victorious and the federal government again ruled all the states.

above: Queen Victoria of England

above: Commodore Perry, the American naval officer who persuaded the Japanese to open their country to foreign trade

Historical Pictures Service, Chicago

Historical Pictures Service, Chicago

The American Civil War
Battle of Gettysburg

Unfortunately, soon after the conflict was ended, President Abraham Lincoln was assassinated. The hard terms of peace forced on the South by men less charitable and able than Lincoln left hard feelings for years to come.

Still the nation was growing and expanding toward the west. Soon the continent was crossed by a railroad that made it possible to ship goods from east to west and the country built up a thriving business life. As a result of the new strong government and good business life, the American nation soon would begin to extend its influence and trade around the world.

The Industrial Revolution

In the seventeenth century, the people of the world did not have many conveniences. They made their own tools to farm the land. They made their clothes at home. There were no steam engines, steamboats, telegraphs, or bicycles. People had never heard of a trolley car or seen a room light up when a switch was touched. They had never even imagined a moving picture, an automobile, an airplane, a radio, or a television set.

Man needed machines, and when man needs something, he usually finds a way to invent it. About 1750, scientists and inventors began to use their talents and a change started to take place. Men began to develop crude machinery to make new kinds of goods. This development started what is known as the *Industrial Revolution*. The Revolution started in England during the second half of the eighteenth century but spread to every nation in the world.

The first developments came with a series of inventions in the textile industry. The spinning wheel was replaced by a machine called the *spinning jenny* that could make many threads at one time instead of just one. The machine was small and could be used in workers' cottages.

The next machine was called a *water frame*. It was so huge and so heavy that it had to be put in a place big enough to hold it. This started the system we know today as the factory. Before the growth of factories, most work was done by hand. But handmade goods could not be produced fast enough for hand-workers to compete with machines.

Under the factory system machines were used and people worked for wages. Articles were made in large quantities and usually a worker did only a certain part of the job. Other workers finished it.

Samuel Crompton took the spinning jenny and the water frame and came up with a machine called a *mule* that could spin very fine thread.

A *power loom* was invented by Edmund Cartwright. This machine automatically wove into cloth the thread spun by the other machines.

With so many new spinning and weaving machines, cotton was in great demand. English factories needed more and asked the cotton growers in the southern part of the United States to send them their crops.

Thus America entered the Industrial Revolution. In 1793 a schoolteacher named Eli Whitney visited a plantation in Georgia and saw the problem of the cotton grower.

Whitney was only an amateur inventor, but he decided to build a machine that could separate the seed from the cotton much faster than could be done by hand. He called it a *cotton gin*. His first gin was crude but it could seed cotton ten times faster than a person could.

America began to advance and prosper. Transportation and communication inventions were the next phase of the Industrial Revolution. Up to this time men traveled by horse and wagon on land and by sailboat on the sea.

James Watt was one of the first inventors to change this. Watt had watched a boiling kettle on the stove and noticed that the steam lifted the lid. This gave him an idea that steam might lift other things as well as the lid of a teakettle. So he made a machine in which steam lifted a lid called a piston in such a way that a wheel was turned. This was the first *steam engine*.

Watt's steam engine moved wheels and other things, but it didn't move itself. An Englishman named Stephenson put Watt's engine on wheels and made the engine move its own wheels. This was the first *locomotive*. Soon carriages drawn by engines were made to run on tracks in America. At first these trains ran only a few miles out from such cities as Baltimore and Philadelphia.

Then a young man named Robert Fulton thought he could make a boat go by putting Watt's engine on board and making it turn paddle wheels. People laughed at him and called the boat he was building "Fulton's Folly," which means "foolishness." But the boat worked, and Fulton had the last laugh. He called his boat the *Clermont*, and it made regular trips up and down the river.

No one had ever been able to communicate with anyone far away until an American painter named Morse invented a wonderful instrument called the *telegraph*. In the telegraph, electricity flows through a wire from one place to another place which may be a long distance off. If a button is pressed at one end of the wire, the electricity stops flowing through the wire, and the instrument at the other end makes a click. A short click is called a dot, and a long click is called a dash. These dots and dashes stand for letters of the alphabet, and messages can be spelled out by dots and dashes. Morse built the first telegraph line in America between Baltimore and Washington.

A schoolteacher named Bell was trying to find some way of making deaf children hear, and in so doing he invented the *telephone*. The telephone carries words in the same way the telegraph carries clicks.

Many things now in everyday use have been partly invented by several people, so that it is hard to say just which one thought of the invention first. Several people thought of a way to run a machine by feeding it electricity. This was the electric motor. Then others thought of a way to run a machine by exploding gas. This was the motor used in automobiles.

Electric lights, such as we use indoors, were invented by Thomas Alva Edison. He also invented many things connected with the phonograph and the movies.

Thousands of people who lived in past ages tried to fly and failed. Millions of people said it was impossible to fly and foolish to try. At last, after long years of work and thousands of trials, two American brothers named Wright did the impossible. They invented the airplane and flew.

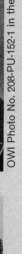
OWI Photo No. 208-PU-152-1 in the National Archives

Historical Pictures Service, Chicago

opposite top: Robert Fulton, inventor of the steamship

opposite bottom: Samuel Morse, inventor of the telegraph

top right: Alexander Graham Bell, inventor of the telephone

bottom right: Thomas Alva Edison, inventor of the electric light

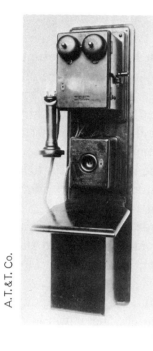

above, left to right:

Fulton's steamship, the *Clermont,* on the Hudson River

One of the first telephones built

Edison's first electric lamp

Model of the *Britannia,* a steamship built about thirty-five years after Fulton's *Clermont*

The illustration below shows the Wright brothers preparing to make their historic
flight at Kitty Hawk, North Carolina

Colonial Expansion

During the late nineteenth and early twentieth centuries, the desire for colonial expansion again became important. Most of the new lands now acquired by countries were obtained for economic reasons. Colonies could supply the mother country with new materials and in turn could buy finished goods from her. These new lands also were useful as military bases and for providing opportunities to new settlers. Added to this were the patriotic ideas and religious feelings that prompted many missionaries, teachers, doctors, and others to explore and settle in faraway lands.

In the scramble for land and power Africa became a land divided. Belgium colonized the Congo. France did the same in Algeria, Tunis, French Sudan, West Africa, Morocco, and French Equatorial Africa.

After the defeat of Napoleon, England took Cape Colony on the tip of South Africa from the Dutch. Her power was extended in 1882 to Egypt and the Sudan in northern Africa. Then after a three-year war with the Boers—Dutch settlers in South Africa—she added more land.

Germany and Italy also joined this quest for more land. Germany established many colonies in Africa—Kanerun, Togoland, Southwest Africa, and East Africa. Italy took over Eritrea, Somaliland, Tripoli, and Abyssinia.

Powers in the East continued to land grab. In 1907, Persia was divided between Russia and England. China was next—and was opened by force. England was first to fight. Other nations joined in until by 1900 different areas in China were controlled by different powers—Russia, Germany, England, France, and Japan.

In her brief war with Spain, America gained colonial possessions in the Caribbean and the Pacific.

These world powers competed with each other continuously. Despite the growing troubles, major wars were avoided. But the stage was set, for sides were being taken, armies were being built up and leaders were growing impatient for undisputed power.

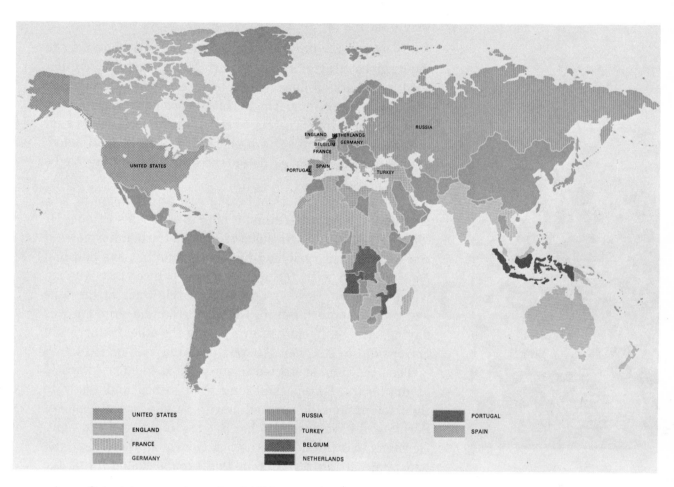

UNITED STATES
ENGLAND
FRANCE
GERMANY

RUSSIA
TURKEY
BELGIUM
NETHERLANDS

PORTUGAL
SPAIN

ENGLAND NETHERLANDS
BELGIUM GERMANY
FRANCE
PORTUGAL SPAIN
TURKEY
RUSSIA
UNITED STATES

above: Colonial possessions about 1900

opposite: Military rule was used by European powers to keep the peace in foreign territories

below: Administration buildings like this were headquarters for European powers in many lands

A World at War: 1914–1918

above: The assassination of Archduke Ferdinand; the shot fired at this time touched off World War I.

opposite top: World War I air battle

opposite bottom: American troops march through a shattered village in France during World War I

There was a small country in Europe called Serbia, next to the large country of Austria. Serbia and Austria were not good neighbors because Serbia believed that Austria ruled her kingdom unfairly. The Serbians formed secret societies to send people into Austria to stir up trouble. Austria said that Serbia was trying to break up the Austrian kingdom by making the people discontented and unwilling to be ruled by Austria.

Then a young man from Serbia shot an Austrian prince, Archduke Francis Ferdinand, heir to Austria's throne. Of course Austria was furious and blamed Serbia. Serbia said she was very sorry it had happened but that she had had nothing to do with the death of the prince. But Austria wouldn't accept Serbia's apology. Austria thought the time had come to punish Serbia for all the trouble Austria was having. And so, in spite of everything the other countries in Europe did to stop her, Austria declared war in 1914.

Then the trouble started to spread just like fire in a field of dry grass. Europe had long been armed and ready to fight for national honor and power. Russia took the side of Serbia and gave orders to her armies to get ready to fight. Germany took the side of Austria. Nearly all these countries had been getting together in two groups, made up of the friends of Germany and the friends of France.

Russia was a friend of France by an agreement made in 1894. So when Russia got ready to fight, France ordered her armies to get ready to help Russia. That meant Germany would be caught between two big enemies—France on one side and Russia on the other. Germany decided to strike quickly at France and destroy her before Russia could hit hard from the other side.

To get at France quickly, Germany had to go through the little country of Belgium. Germany and France both had agreed that neither would march armies through Belgium, but when the war began, her armies marched in anyway and pushed aside the Belgians, who tried to stop them. Germany's armies rushed on toward Paris, the capital of France. The Germans got as far as a little stream called the

102

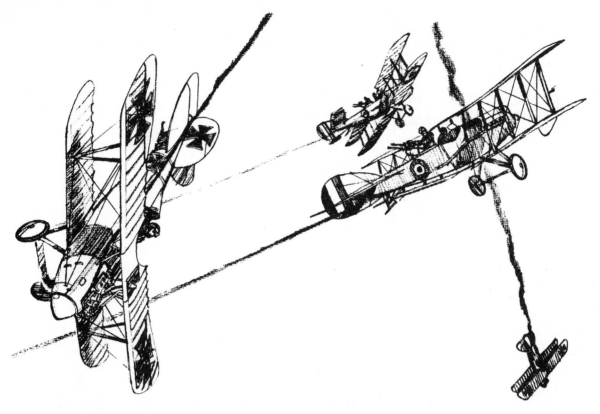

Marne, only twenty miles from Paris. But there the French, under General Joffre, stopped her army. This battle of the Marne is probably the most famous of all the battles you have heard about so far in this history, for though the war went on for four years after this battle, if the Germans had won at the Marne they would have captured Paris and would probably have made France a German country.

But this time England had come into the war on the side of France, Russia, and Belgium, for she had signed agreements with these nations between 1904 and 1907. England had the strongest navy in the world. The German navy wasn't strong enough to beat the English navy and so Germany kept her battleships at home. She had to fight from under the sea with submarines, which were hard for the English ships to catch. It was the first war in history in which battles were fought not only on land and on sea but up in the air and down under the water.

The German submarines sometimes sank ships belonging to countries that weren't in the war. That, of course, made these countries very angry with Germany and so before the war was over nearly all the countries of the world were in the fight. That is why it is called a World War. The countries fighting against Germany—France, England, and Russia—were known as the Allies.

Millions of people were killed, millions of soldiers were wounded, billions of dollars were spent and still the war went on, with neither side able to win. Then all of a sudden Russia had a revolution. The Russian people refused to fight, for they were too busy with their revolution at home. Things began to look bad for England and France.

The United States did not enter the war until 1917, almost three years after it had begun; then she did so because German submarines were sinking American ships and killing Americans.

At last Germany and her friends surrendered, and on November 11, 1918, Germany signed a paper agreeing to do everything the Allies asked. The kaiser went to live in Holland, and Germany became a republic. Big Austria became little Austria, for all her lands and her people who weren't Austrians were taken away from her and made into independent countries. Serbia disappeared altogether and in her place Yugoslavia was formed.

Boom, Depression, and Revolution

When World War I ended, people everywhere hoped and prayed that there would be no more wars. The war was called the War to End Wars. When World War I ended, the leaders of the Allied governments met at Versailles in France and drew up a peace treaty known as the Treaty of Versailles. The treaty said that Germany could have a small army—an army big enough to keep order in Germany but not big enough to fight a war. There were to be no army or navy airplanes in Germany and no tanks. The treaty also said that Germany would have to pay large sums of money to the Allied nations to help pay for what had been destroyed during the war.

To keep the peace, the League of Nations was set up with headquarters in Switzerland. Since history began, people have tried to find some way to keep wars from starting. People hoped the League of Nations would be the great invention that would keep wars from breaking out. Each country was to send representatives to the meeting of the League. When war threatened, the League would warn the warlike country and ask it to bring its case before the judges of a World Court and let them settle the trouble there instead of having the question decided by war.

The League of Nations didn't succeed. There were several reasons for this. One was that the United States decided not to join the League. This was because a group of American leaders did not want their nation to become involved again in European affairs.

Another reason why the League didn't work was that there was no way the decisions of the World Court could be enforced. The nations had no system set up to make other nations do what the court told them to do. They could only ask that the nations do what it wanted them to do.

Never before did so many people hope and pray that war could be stopped. Other ways to stop wars, besides the League of Nations, were tried too. People thought that if nations were not so heavily armed it might help. So the countries with the biggest navies held a conference in Washington, D.C., and agreed to limit the size of their navies.

People also thought that if all the countries of the world solemnly promised not to make war, they might keep their word; so an agreement called an Anti-War Treaty was made. Sixty-two countries signed this treaty and promised to give up war.

Yet wars did break out again—in spite of the League of Nations, in spite of limiting the navies, in spite of the Anti-War Treaty. There was no force in the world that could be used to stop a war when one started. And so, the twenty year period between world wars was not free from war. The first new war was in Asia.

The island country of Japan had changed to modern ways after Commodore Perry had opened her to foreign trade. Japan had learned the bad things as well as the good things of Western civilization. She had built a large, modern army and navy. In 1931, Japan used her army to take away from China the northern part of the country, called Manchuria. Later the Japanese tried to take over all of China. Of course the Chinese fought the Japanese.

But no other country tried to stop the Japanese by force and the war continued. The Chinese fought hard but they had very few military supplies, and soon Japan had taken all the eastern coast of China and driven the Chinese government into western China. The League of Nations couldn't stop this war and it was still going on when World War II started.

While this war between China and Japan was going on in Asia, another war had started in Africa. The Italian army marched into the ancient country of Ethiopia. The Ethiopian army had a few guns, but most of their soldiers were armed with spears. The Italians used airplanes, bombs, artillery, and even poison gas, and soon conquered the Ethiopians.

Next a civil war broke out in Spain between the loyalists who wanted a king and the republicans who wanted to abolish the monarchy. Instead of trying to stop the war, Russia sent soldiers to help the republicans and Germany and Italy sent soldiers to help the loyalists. Germany and Italy used Spain as a testing ground to get their men and machines ready for what was to follow.

One, two, three—war, war, war—China, Ethiopa, Spain. The League of Nations hadn't been able to stop the Japanese from attacking China, and it couldn't keep Italy from taking Ethiopia. It tried to punish Italy by stopping other countries from sending supplies to Italy, but Italy took Ethiopia anyway. The League had also not been able to stop the war in Spain. As an invention for stopping wars or preventing them, the League of Nations was a dismal failure.

Other events of worldwide importance occurred during the twenty-year period between World War I and World War II. During this time a revolutionary form of government was to gain control in Russia and influence the future history of the world.

The type of government established in Russia in 1917 was based on the ideas of a man named Karl Marx. Marx, a German writer, was horrified by the poor living conditions of the poor. He felt that the profits from the factory systems were not being fairly distributed, and that one group got everything. The wealthy were priviledged and led a comfortable life. The poor were left out almost entirely.

In an attempt to solve this problem, Marx wrote a book. Here he presented a new government that he believed would correct the situation. He said that the workers were the most important people in any country. Production—the making and growing of things—was the most important activity of any country. So he felt the workers should revolt and set up a system in which the government would own the farms, factories, and businesses. Then everyone in the country would get from the government just as much as they needed. They would all be equal—no one person would get more than another.

Marx also said that governments could be changed only by revolution. The workers must force others to accept this new way of life. Then after one successful revolution, the system must be brought to every nation in the world, using force if necessary.

This idea of government is known as Communism. People who believe in this system are called Communists. The people in Russia who wanted Communism were called Bolsheviks (bowl' she-vihks) or Communists.

Not long after the beginning of the revolution and the assassination of the czar, the government was taken over by a man named Lenin. Leading the Bolsheviks, Lenin began to silence all opposition to Communism. There was a civil war in Russia, and at the end of three years of fighting, the Communists were victorious. Peace was established and the Communists began to rebuild their nation.

Lenin's government was based on Marx's teachings. Property was taken over by the state, or government, to be used by all the people. Most of the big farms that had once belonged to the czar and his nobles were broken up. Each farmer was allowed to work as much land as he could farm himself. The farmer then gave the crop to the state.

Eventually the state took from all individual owners the right to own any store, factory, or business. Even the name of the country was changed. It was renamed the Union of Soviet Socialist Republics, which is frequently shortened to U.S.S.R. Russia was beginning a new way of life, completely different from what it had been during the rule of the czars.

A constitution was written that set up a lawmaking body for the U.S.S.R. The lawmakers were elected by the people. The constitution was written to protect the rights of individuals. The U.S.S.R. seemed to be establishing a democratic government. But this was not so. The leaders of the Communist party made all the laws and had all the power. The men elected under the constitution were simply puppets. Lenin was actually a dictator.

When Lenin became dictator there was much suffering. Many people were starving and many who were not in favor of Communism were shot or exiled to cold Siberia. But more and more schools were built, and this was good, for few people had been able to go to school when the czars had ruled. The poor people were still poor, but they felt now that there was a great difference from being poor under the czar with no hope of a better life. Now they felt the government was their government. There was hope of better things to come. Great dams were built across the rivers to supply electricity for steel plants and tractor factories. The nobles' palaces were turned into museums for the people. Subways were built in Moscow. The army was given good leaders and was well trained.

But the Communists did things that worried other countries. They made the Christian religion unlawful and closed all the churches. And although they said they had a workers' government, the workers really didn't get many personal gains, the power and wealth remained in the

Lenin, the dictator of Russia after the revolution

hands of only a few. Also, the Communists believed that Communism should be spread all over the world. Even in countries where the people were not ill-treated and were satisfied with their own kind of government, the Communists hoped to start revolutions so that Communism could be the form of government everywhere.

When Lenin died in 1924, there was a struggle between two top government officials, Stalin and Trotsky, over who would be the new dictator. The man who took Lenin's place as the ruler, or dictator of Russia was called by his nickname, Joseph Stalin, which means "man of steel." He was a man of steel and nothing stopped him from getting what he wanted. Any man who disagreed with him was killed or disappeared. Stalin wanted to build a strong country and spread Communism.

Under Stalin the Russians built more factories and even large new cities where the factories would do the most good. Collective farms were started. Starvation, execution, or slave-labor camps awaited anyone who refused to give up his land. A collective farm is a large farm where everybody works together to raise the crops and the profit goes partly to the government and partly to all the people on the collective farm. No one person owns any land; the land belongs to the government.

Historical Pictures Service, Chicago

Joseph Stalin ruled Russia as dictator for over twenty-five years

Under the Communists, Russia has made many advances in building, manufacturing, and transportation. But not in liberty or freedom. Russia is ruled by dictators. People are not allowed to do or say what they want, but only what the government wants. Only Communists can hold office. There is only one party from which Russian citizens select their leaders. The newspapers in Russia are not and never have been free to print the news they want to print, but must print only what the government tells them to print. Visitors from other countries are not welcome in the U.S.S.R., and very few Russians are allowed to visit other countries.

The biggest country in the world has now become one of the most important and powerful countries. It is a dangerous enemy of the democratic Western world, because the dictators in Russia still feel that all governments should be communistic.

During the time Russia was developing its new government, people in the rest of the world were busy making and selling and buying and using the peacetime things they had not been able to enjoy while the war was going on. In the

United States, almost everyone who wanted to work could get a job. Factories were busy turning out everything from clothespins to automobiles. Business was booming; people were making money and spending it.

Many people thought these good times—called a *boom*—would go on forever, but they were wrong. The boom didn't last. What businessmen call a *depression* followed the boom. Good jobs became scarce. Millions of people could not get jobs at all. Factories could not sell as many things as they could make. Many factories had to close. This caused more people to be without jobs. And men could not get money to buy food for themselves and their families if they couldn't find jobs. The last ten years of the peace were troubled times of depression in America and Europe.

The depression had been going on in America for three years and people were getting desperate when a new President, Franklin Delano Roosevelt, was elected. He became president just when the depression seemed hopeless, and when everything looked black and gloomy.

Then the government hired thousands of people to work in any way they could. Roosevelt tried out many new ways to get business back to normal and help the common man. The changes he made became known as the New Deal.

Roosevelt was president from 1933 to 1945. No other man had been president more than eight years, nor been elected more than twice. Roosevelt had been elected four times in a row.

Roosevelt wasn't able to stop the depression right away. He did show people that everything wasn't hopeless, and he did keep people from going hungry and perhaps starving, but it cost the government millions and millions of dollars.

Before Roosevelt's third term had begun, the twenty years of peace were over—World War II had started in Europe. The people of the United States hoped their country could keep out of this war, but Roosevelt felt that America might be attacked even though the war was far away across the ocean. He prepared the country for war in case it came, and when the United States was attacked Roosevelt led the country through the war to victory against Italy, Germany, and Japan. He died a month before the Germans surrendered.

Franklin Roosevelt, as President of the United States, guided the country through the depression and World War II

World War II

Italy had a king, Victor Emmanuel, but the real ruler of the country was a man named Mussolini who had become dictator some years after the end of World War I. It was Mussolini who led Italy into war with Ethiopia.

The people of a country run by a dictator are seldom really happy because they have to do whatever the dictator tells them to do whether they like it or not. People must be careful what they say for fear of saying something the dictator might not like. They may be imprisoned without a trial; they cannot read about both sides of an issue in their newspapers, for the newspapers print only what the dictator wants them to print. People are always afraid in a dictatorship, for the dictator's spies are always listening and watching and waiting for someone to make a slip—to say something against the dictator or do something he might not like.

Mussolini was bad enough. He took away the liberties of the people in Italy. He made war on the Ethiopians just because he wanted their country. But Mussolini was not nearly as bad as another dictator who came to power in Europe—Adolf Hitler, who became the dictator of Germany. Hitler's followers called themselves Nazis, which was a word made up of the initial letters of the German words for National Socialist German Labor Party.

The Nazis were brutal and cruel. They did horrible things that even the barbarians of the Dark Ages hadn't done.

The Nazis hated Jews, and persecuted the Jews of Germany. Some of the Jews escaped to other countries, but those who could not get away were put in concentration camps where many of them were tortured and killed. As the Nazis conquered more and more of Europe, they persecuted the Jews wherever they went. They built large gas chambers, which were big rooms into which poison gas could be piped. They crowded Jews—men, women, and children—into these chambers and turned on the gas. In this way the Nazis murdered six million Jews.

Not only Jews but thousands of other people in Germany who were thought to be against the Nazis were sent to concentration camps where many of them died.

Historical Pictures Service, Chicago

Benito Mussolini was dictator of Italy during World War II

Adolf Hitler, chancellor of Germany and leader of the Nazis

Hitler became Chancellor (prime minister) of Germany in 1933. He was a great speaker and by his speeches he could move his listeners to do anything he wanted, but he did not depend only on his speeches. His Nazi spies were everywhere and anyone who said a word against him was likely to be arrested by the Nazi secret police—the Gestapo.

Hitler wanted to make Germany the most powerful nation in the world. To do this he started to build a huge army. Everyone in Germany was supposed to help make the Germans a warlike nation.

The Treaty of Versailles did not allow the Germans to have a big army or any air force at all, but Hitler said that Germany was not bound by the Treaty of Versailles—even though it had been signed by the German government. The Germans under Hitler started to take land from other countries. Their army marched into Austria and made Austria a part of Germany. Then they took first a part, and then all of Czechoslovakia. Hitler managed to take two whole countries and no one even tried to stop him!

England and France had a treaty with Poland, which is the country next to Germany on the east. This treaty with Poland said that England and France would protect the independence of Poland, so when Germany threatened to attack Poland, England and France warned Germany about the treaty and said it was their duty under the treaty to protect Poland. But Hitler went ahead and attacked Poland anyway. First he sent his airplanes to bomb Poland; then came the German army with its guns and tanks. The Polish army was much smaller than the German army and had no modern weapons. Hitler conquered Poland in less than four weeks. Germany invaded Poland on September 1, 1939. England and France declared war on Germany and World War II began.

Russia was on the other side of Poland, and Russia marched into Poland from her side. Germany had made a secret agreement to give Russia part of Poland if Russia wouldn't interfere. The nation of Poland ceased to exist.

Next Germany attacked Norway and Denmark. Norway was invaded by airborne German soldiers who were helped by a few traitors in Norway.

Then Germany attacked France through Belgium and Holland. The German airplanes and tanks were too much for the French, Belgian, and Dutch armies, and the English army that had been sent to France to help them. As soon as Mussolini saw that the Germans were winning, he brought Italy into the war on the side of Germany. Soon Holland and Belgium and most of France were taken by the Germans. The German army marched into Paris. Thousands of Frenchmen were sent to work as slaves in Germany, and only England was left to fight the Nazis.

When France was defeated, the English leader, Neville Chamberlain was forced to resign as prime minister and Winston Leonard Spencer Churchill was elected. Winston Churchill was a truly great man. He made speeches over the radio to the people to encourage them to fight on in spite of all the odds against them. Churchill said, ". . . We shall defend our Island, whatever the cost may be. We shall fight on the beaches, we shall fight on the landing grounds, we shall fight in the fields and in the streets, we shall fight in the hills; we shall never surrender . . ."

The Nazis prepared to invade England. They brought more than three thousand barges to the coast of France and Belgium, opposite England, to carry Nazi soldiers across the English Channel. Nazi planes were sent over in great fleets to bomb the English airfields and seaports.

Then Hitler met his first defeat in what was called the Battle of Britain. The English had fewer planes but they were able to outfight the Nazi planes. In the first ten days of this air battle the English shot down 697 German planes and lost only 153 of their own.

When Hitler found that his planes could not destroy the English air force, he sent fleets of airplanes day and night to bomb London, hoping to make the people want to end the war. Thousands of London civilians were killed by these German bombs and much of the city was destroyed, but still the English anti-aircraft gunners and the Royal Air Force kept shooting down so many German planes that at last the Germans were afraid to send planes over England except at night. All during the war these night raids on English cities continued, but Hitler had lost his chance to invade England. The English had had time to obtain weapons and build up their army. Prime Minister Churchill said of the English airplane pilots, "Never in the field of human conflict was so much owed by so many to so few."

U.S. Army Photo

Winston Churchill, a man of many talents, served as prime minister of England during World War II

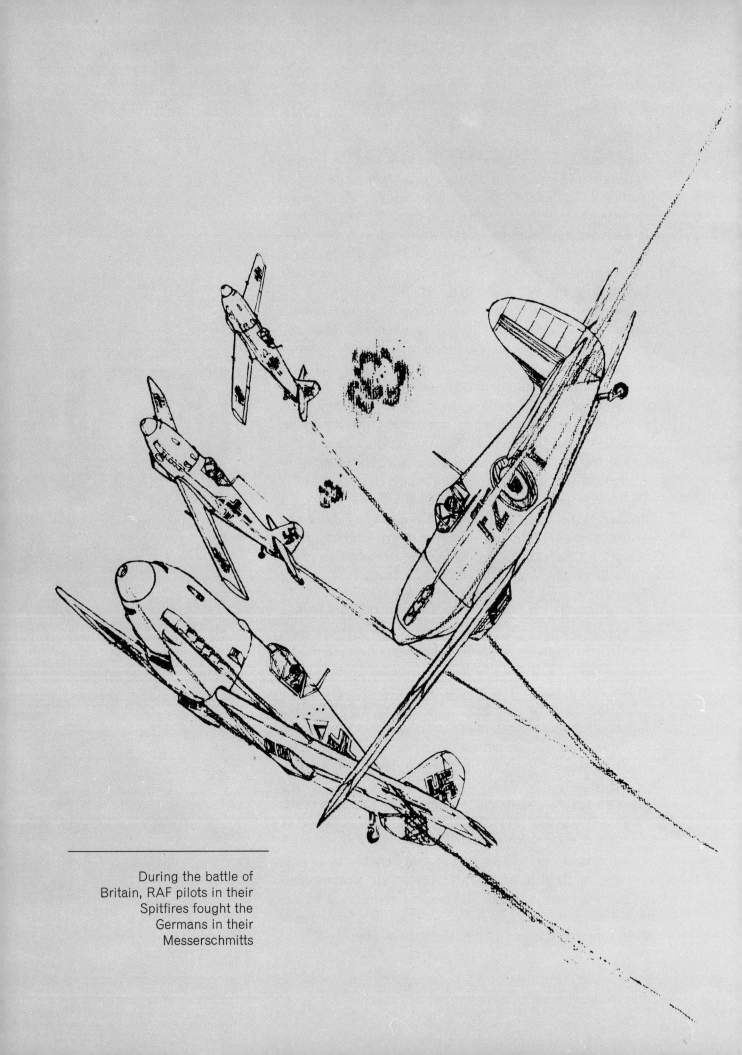

During the battle of
Britain, RAF pilots in their
Spitfires fought the
Germans in their
Messerschmitts

Allied Victories

After the fall of France, only the British Empire—of all those countries that Germany had attacked—was left unconquered. They refused to give up and kept right on trying to beat the most powerful, the best-trained, and best-equipped army in the world.

Men came to fight for their mother country from every corner of the British Empire: Canadians, Australians, Indians, South Africans.

Mussolini had brought Italy into the war on the side of Germany, Japan was still fighting in China, and Japan was friendly to Germany. Germany, Italy, and Japan were known as the Axis powers and together they thought they could conquer the world.

Even the United States, thousands of miles across the ocean from Europe and Japan, felt that its defenses should be strengthened. The small American army was greatly enlarged and American factories were put to work making tanks and airplanes and other war supplies. New ships were built for the navy. A large modern army, however, cannot be raised and trained and equipped in just a few days. It takes not days, nor months, but years—and it takes even longer to build warships than it does to build an army. It was lucky for America that President Roosevelt led the country in preparing itself for war when he did, because just about a year later America was attacked without warning—and even then the country wasn't ready.

While the Germans were still busy setting up their rule in France, Denmark, and Norway and were trying to subdue England from the air, Italy tried to capture Greece and Egypt. But the Italian army was not as good as the German army. The brave Greeks held off the Italians there while an English general in North Africa, using soldiers from all parts of the British Empire, beat two Italian armies that had five times as many soldiers as he had. This freed Ethiopia from the Italians.

Then the Germans sent an army to Greece that conquered the country in only three weeks. They also sent to North Africa an army that fought the British there for the next three years.

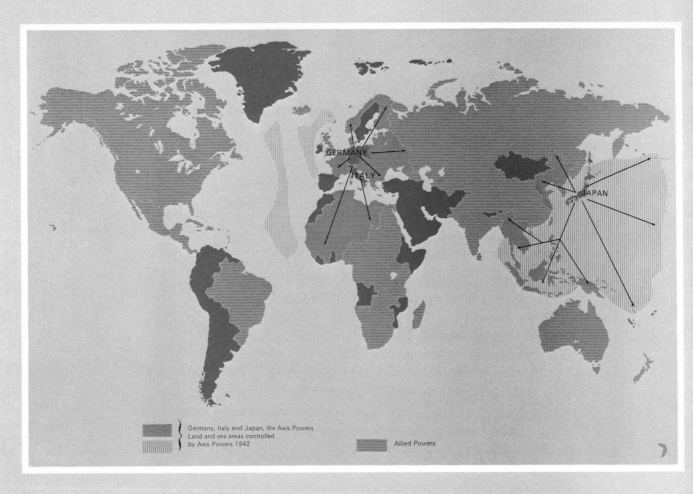

Germany, Italy and Japan, the Axis Powers
Land and sea areas controlled
by Axis Powers 1942

Allied Powers

Map of Axis powers
at their height

Suddenly Hitler attacked Russia. Hitler knew that if he conquered Russia, Germany would gain great quantities of oil, wheat, lumber, and minerals. Besides, he thought Russia might attack Germany, for Russia had been building up a big army ever since the Nazis had started their conquests. Hitler by now had brought fifteen European countries under Nazi rule, and his armies had never been beaten, though his air force had not been able to make England surrender.

The Germans attacked with a mighty rush, hoping to destroy the Russian armies quickly. Far into Russia the Nazis fought, but the Russian armies, though driven back, were not destroyed. Finally the Nazis reached Moscow and attacked the city on three sides at once. Hitler announced that the battle of Moscow would be the deathblow of the Russian armies—but he spoke too soon. The Russians held Moscow for weeks against Germans, who attacked with thousands of tanks and airplanes. Russian soldiers and the

116

civilians of the city fought side by side to defend it. Finally the Russians pushed back the German army. Moscow was saved.

Keeping the Germans from taking Moscow, however, would not be enough to win the war, just as keeping them out of England wouldn't win the war. Germany and Italy still held almost all of Europe.

Then, just as the Russians were driving back the Nazis from Moscow, Japan struck. On December 7, 1941, Japanese airplanes—without any warning at all—bombed the American fleet in Pearl Harbor, Hawaii. Many American warships were sunk or damaged and more than two thousand Americans were killed. Four days later Germany and Italy declared war on the United States.

The United States still was not ready to fight both Germany and Japan at the same time. Her new armies were not yet trained, and a new fleet was not yet ready to take the place of the ships sunk at Pearl Harbor. It was a good thing Russia was fighting fiercely in Europe, for this kept millions of Nazis occupied there and gave America another year to get ready. The United States sent tanks and trucks and other supplies to Russia and to the British army in Egypt—as fast as American factories could make them and ships could carry them.

Japan, however, could not be stopped. The Japanese captured the Philippine Islands, which belonged to the United States. They captured the great British naval base of Singapore in Malaya. They captured the islands of the East Indies that belonged to Holland. They captured Thailand and Burma and pushed on toward India. They captured the Malay Peninsula. They had already seized French Indochina (now the countries of North and South Viet Nam, Laos, and Cambodia) and much of China.

Look at these places on the map to see how far Japan's armies went in Asia. On the map you can find the islands of the Pacific Ocean they captured—islands far from Japan, islands with strange names you would never hear about in a history book except for the battles that were fought there in World War II: Guam and Wake, New Guinea, Bougainville and Guadalcanal, Kiska in the Aleutians.

Many of the places the Japanese captured were defended bravely. The Philippines were taken only after the American and Philippine soldiers all were either killed or captured, except a few who escaped to the hills where small bands of guerrillas kept on fighting as best they could.

President Roosevelt and Prime Minister Churchill had decided to defeat Hitler first and then concentrate on Japan, so the American and British armies invaded North Africa. They fought and beat the German army there. Next, they crossed the Mediterranean and attacked Sicily and Italy.

After the invasion of Italy great numbers of American and British soldiers were assembled in England. From England airplanes bombed Germany and fought the German air force. Finally, on June 6, 1944, all was ready for the invasion of France. A huge force of American and British soldiers under the command of General Dwight Eisenhower crossed the English Channel and landed on the coast of Normandy in France. They fought the Germans in fierce and bloody battles and chased them back across France to Germany. France, Belgium, and Holland were freed and became independent countries again.

In the meantime, the Russians—who had been fighting the Germans on the other side of Europe—put on a tremendous drive and pushed the Germans back into Germany. They captured Berlin, the capital city. Mussolini had been caught and shot by the Italians themselves in Italy, and now Hitler, with his armies defeated, killed himself in the ruins of Berlin.

The terrible Nazis at last were beaten, but millions of people were still homeless and hungry and had to be fed with food shipped in from other countries.

On the other side of the world the war against Japan was still going on. Many battles had been fought against the Japanese on land, at sea, and in the air. General Douglas MacArthur was the commanding general of all Allied Forces in the Pacific. One after another the islands Japan had overrun were recaptured by fierce and bloody fighting, often with the heat and diseases of tropical jungles to add to the difficulties of the fighting men. The Allies were ready to invade Japan itself when a terrible new weapon was used against the Japanese, and Japan surrendered.

This new weapon was the atomic bomb. Only two of them were dropped from American airplanes onto two Japanese cities, but they caused such awful destruction that the Japanese realized they could not win.

Germany surrendered in May and Japan in August of 1945. The biggest and most terrible war in the history of the world was over.

The United Nations

After World War I, you remember, most countries of the world joined in a League of Nations to keep new wars from starting; but wars kept right on happening anyway.

After World War II, most countries of the world joined together in a United Nations to try again to keep new wars from starting. The United Nations, like the League of Nations, was formed to help keep peace and security in the world. In 1945, representatives from fifty nations met in San Francisco to plan a charter. A charter gives the aims and purposes of an organization. On June 26, a charter was accepted and signed by each country at the conference. The nations themselves signed and approved the charter by October 24, 1945, which is now celebrated as United Nations Day.

Originally there were fifty-one members in the United Nations. New members are allowed to enter when two-thirds of the members vote to accept them. The United Nations, with headquarters in New York City is divided into six groups or committees. They are the General Assembly, the Security Council, the International Court of Justice, the Economic and Social Council, the Secretariat, and the Trusteeship Council.

The United Nations Seal is a map of the world encircled by two olive branches which signify peace

The General Assembly includes all the member nations. Each nation may have as many as five representatives to the General Assembly but only one vote per nation. This group can discuss any subject except one that is being discussed by the Security Council. The General Assembly may make suggestions to other United Nations bodies or to governments of member nations. Annual, or yearly, sessions are held and sometimes a special session is called. The president is elected from the representatives.

The Security Council has only one job—to keep world peace and security. There are eleven members of this group. Five of the members are permanent members from China, Great Britain, France, Russia, and the United States. The other six are elected by the General Assembly, three each year, for two-year terms. Each member has one vote. Arguments or disputes can be brought before this council for settlement by any member country. The first method used to solve a problem is discussion, reason, and compromise. If this does not work, trade relations or communications may be cut off. If this is unsuccessful, military action may be taken by the forces of the United Nations.

The International Court of Justice is not located in New York, but in The Hague in the Netherlands. Fifteen judges are elected to serve for nine years, five every third year. When two countries are having difficulties, they may bring their case to the International Court of Justice. They do not have to be member nations of the United Nations, but they must agree to accept and act according to the decision of the court. The court also gives legal advice to groups within the United Nations, such as the General Assembly.

The Economic and Social Council is concerned with everything to do with peace—health, education, human rights, culture, and raising standards of living. Eighteen members are selected by the General Assembly. Six are elected each year to serve for three years. Many agencies are under the Economic and Social Council.

UNESCO is the United Nations Educational, Scientific, and Cultural Organization, which tries to help promote education in the world, bring science to all parts of the world, and encourage exchanges of culture.

FAO is the Food and Agriculture Organization of the United Nations, which tries to advance farming, forestry, and fishing and improve nutrition throughout the world.

Many other agencies work through the Economic and Social Council. The Secretariat does the office work necessary for any big organization. It keeps files and does correspondence. The head is called the Secretary General, who is appointed by the General Assembly. The Secretary General is considered the most important single member of the United Nations. He is the chief administrative officer of the United Nations, and represents the United Nations and reports to the General Assembly yearly. Thousands of people work for the Secretary General. If he thinks some countries are in dangerous situations, he can bring the problem to the attention of the Security Council. Since the formation of the United Nations, there have been three Secretary Generals. The first one was Trygve Lie from Norway, the second was Dag Hammerskjöld from Sweden, and the third and present one is U Thant of Burma.

The purpose of the Trusteeship Council is to help those areas of the world that are called trust territories. These trust territories are places that have no government of their own. Through the Trusteeship Council, a member state is appointed as a trustee to help the territory advance and become ready to be independent and have its own government. Since the organization of the Trusteeship Council in 1945, many territories have become independent countries. The first to become independent was Togoland in Africa. Great Britain was the trustee, and in 1957 Togoland became part of the independent country of Ghana.

Many things have been accomplished by the United Nations since it was founded in 1945. After World War II, many Jewish refugees had no place to go. They had no homeland. Through the efforts of the United Nations, the independent state of Israel was formed as a home for these Jewish refugees.

Many of the wonderful things accomplished by the United Nations go almost unnoticed by most people in the world. They don't notice that the United Nations has provided people in some little village in some poor country with better education, medical aid, sanitation conditions, and many other things. These things have happened in many parts of the world.

What has gained attention throughout the world is the work the United Nations has done concerning countries who are fighting, revolting, or trying to resist the spread of Communism. Very often it doesn't appear that the United Nations has been successful in its efforts. But it is hard to imagine what would occur without the advice and intervention of the United Nations in these problems.

One example is Korea. Korea is a peninsula on the continent of Asia. It is not very far from Japan and was under the control of Japan when World War II began. When Japan was defeated, she lost all the lands under her control. Korea was declared independent and was occupied by Russia in the north and the United States in the south. In keeping with their philosophy of spreading Communism, Russia did so in North Korea and finally decided it was time to spread it to South Korea. Korea, for convenience, had been divided along a parallel line, the 38th parallel. In 1950, Communist North Korean forces crossed the parallel, or boundary line, and invaded South Korea. The United States, since they were occupying South Korea, brought the problem to the attention of the Security Council. According to the charter of the United Nations, members were asked to send troops to help keep peace in South Korea. Because these meetings and decisions took time, the North Korean forces had a head start in the war. From 1950 to 1953, bitter fighting went on between the United Nations forces and the North Koreans. A truce was reached in 1953.

To many people, this action in Korea seems to have been useless. But the independence of South Korea was saved and the Communists did not succeed in spreading their beliefs into that part of the world.

Presently, most of the countries in the world are divided into two camps. One group includes the Communist countries led by Russia and China who want to spread their ideas and make all countries communistic, even if they have to do it by force. The other group is made up of all the free countries who want to keep Communism from spreading. Since war and loss of freedom are dreaded by many people, any action taken by the United Nations concerning this problem is watched very closely.

One important problem facing the United Nations today concerns atomic and nuclear weapons. This has been and continues to be discussed. Everyone is trying to come to some agreement that will satisfy all. One idea discussed is disarmament. Disarmament means that all nations would disarm, that is, take apart their weapons so no one would have any. This would be the ideal way to insure peace. The time, energy, money, and equipment now used to develop weapons could then be used to help man.

Other things being discussed by the United Nations are peaceful uses of atomic energy, ways of safeguarding peace, and the exploration of outer space. Their proposal for outer space is that all nations work together in their space efforts rather than individually.

Many parts of the world are considered "trouble spots." These are parts where neighboring countries fight each other from time to time. Turkey and Greece, Israel and Jordan, India and Pakistan, and other neighboring countries in Southeast Asia sometimes have what are called "border incidents," or fighting between their soldiers guarding the frontiers.

Other trouble spots are countries where Communists try to take control. These countries usually have weak governments and unrest among the people. Many of the people are unhappy with their leaders and welcome a change. The Communists watch and when the time is right, they act and try to seize control.

The United Nations is busy trying to prevent both border incidents and revolutionary Communist movements to keep world peace.

Yesterday, Today, and Tomorrow

History is being made every day. It is being made almost every hour. From this point on you will have to read your history in the newspapers and magazines.

Man's struggles, discoveries, and inventions will continue to make what we call history. Already man's inventions seem more magical than magic itself. Airplanes and helicopters take the place of flying carpets. Rocket ships carry cameras and men into the weightlessness of space. Each space achievement provides mankind with information about what has been the unknown. Only about sixty years separate the time of the first balloon and airplane flights from modern-day jet planes and spaceships. This same rapid development has affected many other areas.

New elements have been discovered by scientists. The most impressive of these has been the discovery and use of atomic and nuclear energy. This energy can be used as a destructive force but also it can be used in helpful ways.

Some of the most important discoveries have been about diseases and how to prevent them.

Anesthetics have prevented many people from suffering pain. Many other things have been discovered to prevent disease and to cure people who do get sick.

Many of the inventions are used every day and are hardly noticed as unusual anymore. An electric eye that controls the movement of things such as doors is hardly thought of as unusual anymore. Radar that helps track everything in the sky including storms and tornados is taken for granted.

New discoveries and inventions are being made every day and every hour. We have not mentioned in these books all of the progress man has made in history, nor have we mentioned all man's struggles against war and other enemies such as hunger, disease, and weather.

Our story ends here, but history does not, for history is a continuing story. It is an ever-unfolding record of man— his struggles, his achievements, and his failures.

INDEX: *Young People's Story of the Modern World*

Type   *Century Expanded*
Typesetter   *American Typesetting Corporation*
Printer   *The Regensteiner Corporation*